The

Approval

Detox

Stop Earning Love and Start Receiving It

Belle Titmus

✦Copyright & Disclaimer Page✦

The Approval Detox: Stop Earning Love and Start Receiving It

This book is intended for informational and inspirational purposes only. It does not constitute psychological or medical advice. While written with care and grounded in research and personal experience, this book is not a substitute for therapy, counselling, or professional support. Always consult a qualified health provider for advice tailored to your specific needs.

The author and publisher disclaim any liability arising from the use or misuse of the material contained herein.

First Edition: 2025

✦Acknowledgements✦

This book was born in the tender space between exhaustion and awakening. Though my name lives on the cover, *The Approval Detox* belongs to every soul who ever whispered, *"I just want to be enough."* You are the heartbeat of these pages.

To the brave ones—clients, friends, readers, and fellow recovering pleasers—thank you for teaching me that healing is both a science and a kind of poetry. Your honesty, humor, and wild resilience turned theory into truth.

To my circle—the ones who sent tea, grace, or laughter when sentences refused to behave—thank you for loving me without needing me to perform. You showed me what real belonging sounds like.

To my mentors and the luminous writers whose wisdom steadied my hand—you gave me language for what once felt like chaos.

And to the younger version of me who kept trying to earn love: look what we made by finally stopping the chase.

May this book find you, reader, wherever you're tired of proving. May it remind you that you were always worthy—long before the gold stars, and long after they fade.

Table of Contents

✦Introduction✦

Your Gold Star Isn't God—And Other Truths About the Invisible Addiction

Let's drop the act and cut to the heart of it: approval addiction is the most socially acceptable, gold-star-studded, "good human" hustle you'll ever get tangled up in. And if you're reading this, I'll bet you know the feeling—maybe a little too well.

You know what it is to chase validation like it's oxygen. You know what it's like to get a hit of praise and feel good for a minute—maybe an hour, maybe a day—before the high fades and you're left jonesing for your next fix. Maybe you're the reliable one, the peacemaker, the "sure, I can help" person who's as indispensable as you are invisible. Maybe you're the overachiever, the one who does everything right and still wonders when it'll finally feel like enough.

Here's the kicker: Even when you win the gold star— when you get the applause, the like, the "You're amazing!"—it doesn't stick. You're back at the starting line, hustling for love, belonging, and a feeling of okay-ness you can't seem to hold onto for more than five minutes at a time.

And you're exhausted. Not just physically (though, let's be honest, you'd nap for a week if you could), but emotionally, spiritually, and right down to your nervous system. Because somewhere along the line, you learned that love, safety, and belonging are things you have to earn.

Sound familiar? You're not broken. You're human—and you're in damn good company.

Welcome to the Club No One Admits They Joined

Here's the wild thing: This addiction gets rewarded at every turn. Society loves a people-pleaser. The world throws parades for the selfless, the agreeable, the ones who keep the peace. You get promoted, praised, and patted on the back for being the person who always says yes, always comes through, always makes things easier for everyone else.

But behind that image, there's a cost—a cost nobody talks about because, frankly, it's inconvenient. The cost is your authenticity. Your rest. Your joy. Your sense of being loved for who you are, not what you do.

You might be:

- The "go-to" friend, always available (and always a little bit resentful)
- The fixer, the rescuer, the one who quietly absorbs everyone else's chaos
- The high achiever who can't stop grinding, even as you lose sight of yourself
- The polite one who never makes waves, even as you drown in your own unspoken needs

If any of those sound like you, congratulations—you're not alone. You're just running a program that was never designed to feed your soul.

The Approval Trap: How Did We Get Here?

Let's get honest about how this happens. It usually starts young. Maybe you learned to scan the room for tension before you could spell your own name. Maybe you figured out that being "good," "easy," or "helpful" got you praise (or at least kept you safe). Maybe you noticed that your own needs were inconvenient, or your feelings were "too much," so you learned to swallow them whole.

You became a master at reading the emotional weather, at shape-shifting, at disappearing just enough to keep the peace—but not so much you'd be forgotten entirely. You got good at being what other people needed. The problem? Somewhere along the way, you lost touch with who you actually are.

As an adult, it looks like agreeing to things you hate, apologizing for existing, over-explaining every boundary, and performing "fine" when you're anything but. It looks like living for the next compliment, the next "thanks so much," the next sign that you're okay.

And every time you get the gold star, it feels good—for a second. Then it fades. And the hustle starts again.

What This Book Isn't

This is not a self-help pep talk about not caring what anyone thinks, running off into the sunset of self-love, or weaponizing "authenticity" as an excuse to be an ass.

And this isn't about becoming invulnerable, untouchable, or immune to connection. If you're human, you're wired for community, belonging, and a little bit of admiration. That's normal.

What this book is—a sassy, soul-drenched, science-backed guide to unhooking your worth from the approval machine. It's a reckoning, not a race. A homecoming, not a self-improvement project.

You'll learn to:

- Recognize the roots of your approval addiction (spoiler: it's not your fault)
- Understand how your nervous system got wired for self-abandonment
- Stop performing, over-explaining, and apologizing for your damn existence

- Set boundaries that don't require an apology tour
- Survive the guilt, the backlash, and the detox hangover—and come out brighter
- Reclaim the parts of you that got left behind in the quest to be "good"
- Receive love and praise without shrinking, deflecting, or running for the hills

What You'll Find Inside

Each chapter goes deep—sometimes uncomfortably so—into the psychology, biology, and energetics of approval addiction. You'll get reflection prompts, micro-missions, practical tools, rituals, and mantras for the days when you need a little extra backbone.

You'll discover the "shadow" side of niceness, the hidden payoffs of people-pleasing, and the quantum mechanics of why takers and drama magnets seem to find you every time.

You'll learn how to reparent yourself (without the woo), how to say no without a 400-word disclaimer, and how to let love in without bargaining for it.

And most importantly? You'll come home to the version of you that doesn't have to hustle for love. The version of you that's already worthy, already enough, already allowed to take up space and breathe a full, satisfying, unapologetic breath.

How to Use This Book

Don't rush it. Each chapter is a layer. Some will feel like clarity. Some will sting (that's detox for you). Take breaks. Scream into a pillow if you need to. Celebrate every awkward, honest, imperfect step toward yourself.

Keep a journal close—your truth is going to want somewhere to land.

Above all, remember: You are not bad for wanting love. You are not weak for needing affirmation. But you are allowed to stop contorting for it.

You're allowed to be chosen as-is.
You're allowed to be loved—even when you're not bending.
You're allowed to belong without earning it.

Before We Begin...

If no one has ever told you: The real you—the one underneath the mask, the one that's raw and radiant and sometimes "too much"—is exactly who the world needs.

You don't have to shrink to keep the peace.
You don't have to earn your place at the table.
You don't have to perform for love that was yours all along.

Ready to begin?
Let's detox. Let's reclaim your worth. And let's get free—together.

Part I: The Anatomy of Approval Addiction

✦Chapter 1✦

The Validation Trap

Why Approval Feels Like Oxygen (and Why It's Actually Not)

The Secret Currency of the Approval Economy

Let's start honest: most people are running on approval the way cars run on gasoline. And like fossil fuel, the supply always runs out.
You get a little, burn through it, and go searching for the next fill-up.

You know the cycle.
You bake the perfect cake, crush it at work, or twist yourself into the friend who never needs anything.
Someone says, *"You're amazing!"*
It hits—dopamine fireworks!
And an hour later, you're scanning the horizon for your next fix.

That is the **validation trap**.
It feels like oxygen but behaves like a leash—keeping

you hustling for scraps of approval, never satiated, never still.

This isn't about being "needy" or "insecure."
It's about biology and belonging—ancient wiring running a modern glitch.

Why Approval Became a Drug

Think back to the species' early-access pass to survival. Back then, "belonging" wasn't aesthetics—it was life or death. Get exiled from the tribe, and you didn't just miss Friday plans; you missed protection and dinner. Your nervous system learned: **approval = safety**.

Fast-forward a few millennia, and your brain still fires alarm bells when someone side-eyes a text.
The sabre-toothed tiger is gone, but the wiring stuck. You feel safest in good graces—with family, your boss, your followers, your crush.

It's not a weakness. It's wiring.

Now mix that with the dopamine candy of the digital age—every like, heart, rating, and "Good job!" lights

your brain like a slot machine.
Each hit feels good but fades fast.
And so the chase begins again.

Reflection Break — Where Are You Hustling for Oxygen?

1. Where do you feel the strongest pull to seek approval—work, family, social media?
2. When you imagine disappointing someone, what emotion hits your gut first?
3. What would you do differently if you didn't need anyone's permission?

No judgment—just data. Awareness is detox.

Childhood: Where the Trap Gets Set

Nobody arrives addicted to praise. You learned it.

Maybe home taught you that *"good"* got warmth and *"difficult"* got silence.
Maybe you became the helper, the achiever, the peacekeeper—the kid who kept the emotional weather sunny.

You got skilled at shapeshifting. You read people like barometers.
You learned that being easy kept you safe, and expressive got you exiled.

The script began:

- *If I behave, I'm loved.*
- *If I'm helpful, I belong.*
- *If I'm impressive, I matter.*

And the moral of that story was clear:
Your worth lives in someone else's eyes.

You didn't choose that programming.
But you're the only one who can rewrite it.

The Adult Playground: Fancier Traps, Same Wiring

Now you're grown, probably competent as hell—and tired.
Your résumé sparkles, your relationships look stable, yet you still wake up checking if everyone's happy with you.

Approval addiction in adulthood hides behind productivity, caretaking, and even humor. It sounds like:

- "Was I too much?"
- "Are they mad at me?"
- "Did I do enough?"

It looks like fixing everyone's problems while quietly resenting them.
You keep earning gold stars—but none of them stick.

The Emotional Economy of Approval

Every "yes" against your better judgment is a trade.

You trade **authenticity for acceptance.**
You trade **rest for relevance.**
You trade **truth for temporary peace.**

The exchange rate? Terrible.
Approval is inflationary—its value drops the moment you spend yourself to get it.

You become the emotional vending machine:
everyone presses buttons, you deliver comfort, and

when you're empty, you still apologize for being out of stock.

The True Cost

Let's tally it:

- **Boundaries:** blur into others' needs until "no" feels foreign.
- **Self-trust:** outsourced; you wait for co-signs.
- **Rest:** impossible unless everyone's happy.
- **Joy:** diluted by constant scanning for disapproval.
- **Relationships:** full of admirers, few of witnesses.

And the cruellest loss?
Being liked instead of *being known*.

Why It's So Hard to Quit

Dopamine again—that shiny saboteur.
The more hits you chase, the more tolerance you build. Yesterday's "You're incredible!" becomes today's baseline.
Soon, quiet contentment feels wrong.

This is not moral weakness; it's neurochemical math. You've literally trained your nervous system to measure safety by applause.

But biology can be retrained.
The trap isn't your fault—but it **is** your responsibility to unlock it.

Mini-Detox Mission — Your First Tiny Rebellion

Try one small act of self-loyalty this week:

- Say no without the essay.
- Let someone wait for your reply.
- Share a truth and don't check your phone for reactions.
- Sit with the knot in your stomach and whisper, "I'm still safe."

That discomfort? It's neural re-wiring in progress. Every small defection from approval-chasing loosens the leash.

Reflection Break — Spotting Your Trap

1. Whose opinion still decides how you feel about yourself?
2. What invisible "good" rules do you obey without question?
3. What might collapse—or finally open—if you stopped performing?

Write. Breathe. Don't fix yet—just see.

The Road Ahead

This is the beginning of your **Approval Detox.**

You'll unhook the guilt, update your nervous system, and relearn the difference between *connection* and *compliance.*

By the end, belonging will feel less like performance and more like peace.

Next up, we dive into the invisible curriculum that wrote your "be nice" script in the first place—and start deleting it line by line.

There's nothing wrong with wanting love.

You simply get to want it **without auditioning for it.**

✦Chapter 2✦

Smile, Be Nice, Don't Make Waves

How Childhood Conditioning Trained You to Be Palatable Instead of Powerful

The Invisible Rulebook: You Learn It Before You Can Name It

Before you ever learned your multiplication tables, your nervous system was already memorizing a much more important curriculum: how to stay safe, how to stay loved, and—most of all—how to stay acceptable.

The rules weren't taped to the fridge. They weren't handed out in kindergarten orientation. They were inherited, absorbed, and enforced with a thousand tiny cues:

- The sigh of disappointment when you voiced a strong feeling.
- The extra praise when you were "so helpful."
- The subtle withdrawal when you asserted a need.

- The warmth when you stayed quiet, polite, and easy.

And thus, the first sacred commandment was written on your bones:
Smile. Be nice. Don't make waves.

If you're honest, you probably can't remember not knowing these rules. They're as old as your memory. But here's the secret:
These rules weren't designed to make you powerful. They were designed to make you *palatable*.

Palatable: The Art of Being Easy to Digest

Let's talk about that word. *Palatable.*

It means "easy to take in." Not too strong, not too spicy, not too messy. The palatable child, teen, or adult is the one who is endlessly agreeable, rarely inconvenient, and never, ever "too much."

The problem? Palatability is a recipe for chronic self-abandonment.

Because to be palatable, you have to shrink. You have to sand down your edges, mute your colors, and edit your emotions. You become a master of being "just right"—but never fully yourself.

You become the friend who never asks for help, the partner who never "makes things difficult," the employee who never pushes back, the sibling who keeps the family peace at all costs.

And here's the kicker: the world *loves* you for it. You get praised for being low-maintenance, reliable, sweet, and drama-free.

But inside? You're paying the price in silence, resentment, and a slow erasure of your own selfhood.

Childhood: Where the Script Is Written (and Rehearsed)

Most of us don't choose people-pleasing. We inherit it.

Maybe it started at home:

- You learned that anger was dangerous, so you learned to swallow it.

- You saw that being "good" got you hugs, but being "difficult" got you ignored.
- You discovered that your job was to make things easier for the adults around you—by being the "easy one."

Or maybe it happened at school:

- You got rewarded for sitting still, listening quietly, and coloring inside the lines.
- You noticed that the loud, wild, sensitive, or opinionated kids got labeled as "problems"—so you learned to blend in.

Maybe it came from faith communities, sports teams, or friend groups. Maybe it was cultural, generational, or just plain survival.

Wherever it came from, the message was clear:
Being lovable = being agreeable.
Being safe = being easy to handle.

And so, you got really, really good at performing emotional labor. You managed the moods of the room, anticipated needs before they were voiced, and became the MVP of smoothing things over.

Young you was brilliant. Young you survived.

But the cost? Adult, you can't remember who you are without the script.

The Nervous System: Why "Nice" Feels Like a Survival Skill

Let's take a quick detour into biology.

When you're a child, your nervous system is like a sponge. It soaks up every signal about what is and isn't safe. And because you depend on others for food, shelter, and love, keeping those people happy is a survival instinct—not a personality flaw.

If being expressive, assertive, or emotional brought disapproval or chaos? Your nervous system learned to avoid it. If being helpful, quiet, or agreeable brought connection and calm? Your nervous system learned to seek it.

This is not weakness. It's adaptation.

But here's the kicker:
Your nervous system doesn't automatically update

just because you grow up.

What kept you safe at six can keep you stuck at thirty-six.

How the "Be Nice" Script Shows Up in Adulthood

Fast forward to grown-up life, and the same script plays out:

- You apologize for things that aren't your fault.
- You soften your opinions, or don't share them at all.
- You feel responsible for everyone else's comfort.
- You say yes while your gut is screaming no.
- You replay conversations, worried you were "too much" or "not enough."
- You avoid conflict like it's radioactive.

You become the emotional airbag in every crash. The fixer. The smooth-talker. The one who can be counted on to never "make it weird."

And while everyone else is breathing easy, you're holding your breath.

Because being palatable doesn't actually keep you safe—it just keeps you small.

When Palatability Becomes Armor

Let's name it: the urge to be palatable is armor.

It's a way to avoid rejection, criticism, or abandonment. If you never rock the boat, maybe you'll never be thrown overboard.

But armor is heavy. And the longer you wear it, the more it disconnects you from your own needs, desires, and truth.

You start to forget:

- What you actually want (not just what others want from you)
- What upsets you (not just what you can "handle")
- What lights you up (not just what's acceptable)

You become a curator of comfort for others—a stranger to your own joy.

The Cost of Being "Easy to Love"

Let's get brutally honest about the cost.

- **Self-censorship:** You silence your real feelings to keep the peace.
- **Chronic resentment:** You start to seethe at how little others reciprocate.
- **Invisible labor:** You do the emotional work for everyone, and nobody notices.
- **Loss of intimacy:** No one can truly love you if you're always editing yourself.
- **Emptiness:** You get praise, but it tastes like cardboard.

You start to wonder:

Does anyone actually know me?

Would anyone stay if I stopped being "nice"?

Those questions hurt. But they're also the beginning of freedom.

Reflection Break:

Unmasking the Old Script

Journal gently through these:

1. What behaviors got me the most praise or affection as a child?
2. What traits or emotions did I learn were "too much" for others to handle?
3. What roles did I unconsciously adopt to feel safe in my family, school, or culture?
4. What parts of myself did I have to hide to stay loved?

Then write this truth:

"I am not here to be palatable. I am here to be real."

A Mini Detox Mission: Say the Hard Thing

This week, practice saying one small thing you normally silence, swallow, or sugarcoat.

It might be:

- "That actually hurt my feelings."
- "No, I can't help with that."
- "I need a little space today."
- "That didn't feel fair to me."

You don't have to be dramatic. Just honest.

Your nervous system might shake. That's okay. That's the old story of leaving your body.

The World Needs Your Realness, Not Your Performance

Let's land this gently but firmly:

The world does not need more palatable people.

It needs more real people.

People who can hold discomfort.

People who can say the hard thing.

People who can belong to themselves, even if it costs them approval.

You are not too much. You are not a burden. You are not selfish for needing space, truth, or boundaries.

You are not here to be easy to love.

You are here to be real—and to let real love find *you*.

Micro-Rebellion Practice: Let Yourself Be Seen

This week, show up in your fullness somewhere you normally hold back.

- Wear the outfit that feels a little "extra."
- Share something vulnerable.
- Admit you don't have it all together.
- Let your joy or anger or truth be visible.

When the voice whispers, "You're too much," you get to answer:
"No. I'm finally enough."

Looking Forward: The Next Layer

In the next chapter, we're going under the hood. We'll look at how your nervous system's "fawn" response keeps you stuck in patterns of self-abandonment, and how to start interrupting those patterns—one brave, awkward, liberating moment at a time.

You are not obligated to be palatable, pleasing, or perpetually agreeable.

You are allowed to show up as the full, wild, inconvenient, beautiful human you are.

Let's keep unlearning together.

The Approval Detox

✦Chapter 3✦

The Fawn Response Exposed

How Your Nervous System Got Trained to Seek Safety Through Self-Abandonment

Meet Your Inner Fawn: The Survival Genius in Disguise

Let's get something straight: If you're a chronic people-pleaser, you're not spineless, weak, or lacking in willpower. You're a certified survival genius. Your nervous system is doing exactly what it was built to do—keep you safe. The problem is, your body is working off an old script, and it's time to update the manual.

You've heard of fight and flight, right? Maybe even freeze. But there's a fourth "F" in this trauma survival alphabet, and it's the one nobody talks about: **fawn**.

Fawning is the art of appeasement, the chameleon move, the skillful adaptation that says, "If I can just be what you want, maybe you won't hurt me, leave me, explode, or withdraw." It's the nervous system's version of, "Let's just keep the peace—at any cost."

If you've ever found yourself smoothing, fixing, apologizing, or shape-shifting before you even think, you've met your inner fawn. And if you're reading this, you probably know them intimately.

Survival Instincts: Why Fawning Isn't Your Fault

Let's time-travel back to the beginning. Maybe you grew up in a home where anger was unpredictable, love was conditional, or disappointment was dangerous. Maybe you learned early that fighting back made things worse, and running away wasn't an option. Maybe freezing just prolonged the pain.

So your body got creative. It fawned.
You learned to:

- Sense moods before a word was spoken
- Offer comfort before anyone asked
- Apologize for things that weren't your fault
- Make yourself small, sweet, and "easy" to be around

You didn't choose to be a people pleaser. Your body chose survival. And it did so by wiring your nervous system to equate danger with disapproval and safety with self-erasure.

Every time you successfully avoided conflict by pleasing, your nervous system got a hit of relief: *Ah, we survived. Good job, team.* The loop completed. The groove deepened.

Fast forward a decade or three, and you're saying yes when you want to say no, absorbing everyone else's emotions, and feeling physically sick at the thought of disappointing someone—even if it's just declining a coffee date.

The Science of the Fawn Response

Ready for some nerdy magic? Here's what's happening beneath the surface:

When your body perceives a threat (real or imagined), your amygdala—the brain's security system—lights up. Stress hormones like adrenaline and cortisol surge. Your rational brain goes offline, and your instincts take over.

If fighting or fleeing won't work, your system tries something different:

Fawn. Appease. Make yourself non-threatening.

It's automatic. You don't think, you just do. You smile, soothe, over-accommodate. You become the emotional airbag for everyone else's crash.

And the more you do it, the more your brain wires itself to believe:
"Danger = disapproval. Safety = self-abandonment."

This is not weakness. It's wiring. But wiring can be rewired. That's the good news.

How Fawning Hides in Plain Sight

You might wonder, "Am I really fawning, or am I just nice?"
Here's what fawning actually looks like in everyday life:

- Agreeing when you don't agree, just to avoid conflict

- Anticipating others' needs before they say a word
- Apologizing for existing (saying "sorry" when you want to say "hello")
- Feeling responsible for everyone's moods
- Avoiding sharing your real opinions, needs, or feelings
- Saying yes when your body is screaming no
- Replaying conversations, worried you upset or annoyed someone

To the outside world, you just seem incredibly "nice." Only you know the exhaustion, the anxiety, and the invisible cost.

Who Taught You to Fawn?

You didn't invent this pattern. Someone handed you the script.

Maybe it was a parent who only offered affection when you were "good." Maybe it was a volatile household, where the emotional weather changed in an instant, and your job was to keep the skies clear. Maybe it was a teacher, coach, or faith community that rewarded quiet compliance over honest expression.

Or maybe it was the slow drip of cultural conditioning:
"Don't be difficult."
"Good kids don't make a fuss."
"Be a team player."
"Don't upset your elders."

You learned that appeasement was the cost of belonging. And you paid it, every day.

The Hidden Power of Fawning

Here's a twist: Fawning isn't just about avoiding pain. It's also about wielding influence—controlling the emotional climate by becoming indispensable.

When you make yourself essential to others' comfort, you're not powerless. You're actually running the show (from backstage, of course). You become the fixer, the peacekeeper, the one nobody wants to lose.

But this power comes at a steep price:
You never get to find out who would love you if you stopped performing.

Interrupting the Fawn: The First Brave Steps

So, what do you do when your nervous system is programmed to fawn?
You start by gently, bravely, disrupting the loop. Not with a sledgehammer, but with micro-moves.

Step 1: Notice the Body

Before you say yes, fix, or soothe, pause.
What's happening in your body?
Is your chest tight? Is your stomach clenching? Are you holding your breath?
These are your cues that your fawn reflex is kicking in.

Step 2: Name the Reflex

Silently, to yourself:
"I'm about to fawn right now. My body thinks I'm in danger, but I'm actually safe."
This tiny pause is a radical act of self-awareness.

Step 3: Permission to Pause

You do not have to answer, agree, or apologize immediately.
Try: "Let me think about it and get back to you."
Give your body time to catch up to the present.

Step 4: Test a Tiny "No"

Start small. Say no to something inconsequential—a meeting, a favor, a text.
Feel the discomfort. Notice the world didn't end.

Step 5: Soothe the Aftershock

Fawning withdrawal feels like anxiety, guilt, even grief.
Breathe. Place a hand on your heart. Remind yourself: "I am safe, even if someone is disappointed or uncomfortable."

Reflection Break:

Unlearning the Old Reflex

1. Where in my life do I feel the strongest urge to appease, smooth, or fix?
2. Whose approval feels like oxygen—and what do I fear would happen if I lost it?
3. What physical sensations do I notice when I'm about to people-please?
4. What's one tiny situation this week where I can experiment with not fawning, just for practice?

Write it out. Let honesty (not shame) lead.

Micro-Detox Practice: Ride the Urge, Don't Obey It

This week, when you feel the urge to fawn, pause.
Name it.
Breathe.
See if you can wait 30 seconds before reacting.
Let the urge move through you like a wave—without letting it run the show.

You're not trying to "become selfish."
You're learning to become self-loyal.

You Are Not Your Reflexes—You Are the One Who Rewires Them

Fawning isn't who you are. It's what you learned. And what you learned can be unlearned.

You don't have to trade truth for safety anymore.
You can let your nervous system rest, and your real self rise.

There will be discomfort. There will be guilt. There might even be grief.
But on the other side?
There's breath. There's freedom. And there's the deep relief of finally letting yourself belong—to yourself.

Looking Ahead

In the next chapter, we'll talk about the identity crisis that comes with letting go of the old applause-driven self. What happens when you drop the mask, stop the fawning, and meet the version of you that's been waiting to be chosen—not for performance, but for presence?

You are not a chameleon.
You are not an emotional airbag.
You are not here just to keep the peace.

You are here to be real, to be known, and to be loved as you are.

Let's keep going.

✦Chapter 4✦

Who Would I Be Without the Applause?

Surviving the Identity Crisis When You Stop Performing for Love

When the Applause Stops: Welcome to the Existential Quiet

Let's get honest: The idea of "not needing approval" sounds liberating—right up until the moment someone actually doesn't like you. Then suddenly, the bottom drops out of your stomach, old panic takes the wheel, and you're back in your emotional sandbox, frantically searching for a gold star and a juice box.

This isn't just discomfort. It's an identity earthquake.

Because here's the real heartbreak of people-pleasing: Your self-worth is built on applause, praise, and polite nods from the peanut gallery. When the applause dies down, you're left in a strange, echoing silence that feels less like peace and more like a cosmic "Now what?"

This is the "Who am I without the performance?" moment.

And yes, it's terrifying.

But it is also the birthplace of your real self.

The High of Being Liked (and the Crash That Follows)

Let's not kid ourselves—being liked feels amazing. You nail the presentation, everyone claps, and you're high on sweet, fleeting approval. Or maybe you're the friend who always comes through, the one whose phone lights up with "You're the best!" texts. For a moment, you feel whole. Valid. Necessary.

But here's the hangover: Approval has a short half-life. The high fades, and suddenly you're obsessing:

Did they really mean it?

Am I actually enough?

What if I mess up next time?

You start plotting your next fix before the last one's even worn off.

You are only as good as your last performance, and

the pressure to keep earning love is not just exhausting—it's dehumanizing.

The False Self: The Mask That Outlived Its Usefulness

Let's call it what it is: People-pleasing builds a false self.
A carefully curated avatar designed to be liked, admired, and—above all—never rejected.

You become a social shapeshifter.
In one room, you're the chill friend who never complains.
In another, the high-achiever who stays late and never asks for help.
At home, maybe you're the peacemaker, absorbing everyone else's drama while quietly disappearing.

You get so good at being what others want, you lose track of what you want—or if you ever knew in the first place. You don't just play the part; you become the part.

Until one day, the applause dies down, the audience leaves, and you're left backstage, alone, wondering who the hell you are when no one's watching.

Why Losing Approval Feels Like Dying

Not to be dramatic (okay, maybe a little), but for hardcore people-pleasers, losing approval can feel like a kind of death. And in a way, it is.

The brain is wired for connection. For millennia, being liked meant survival—rejection meant danger, exile, maybe even death. Your nervous system still hasn't gotten the memo that you're not about to be eaten by wolves if someone's disappointed in you.

So when you risk being disliked—by saying no, showing up messy, or refusing to perform—you're not just breaking a habit. You're breaking a primal contract.
It's supposed to feel terrifying.
That doesn't mean you're weak.
It means you're human.

The Collapse Before the Clarity

Here's what most "self-help" books gloss over: When you stop performing for love, you will feel lost. Disoriented. Maybe even a little depressed or empty. That's because you're letting go of the only self you've ever known—the one who survived by being easy, useful, likable.

This, right here, is not failure.
It's the sacred collapse before the clarity.
It's the falling-apart before the coming-together.

You're grieving the version of you that kept you safe for so long. The one who smiled even when your chest was tight. The one who said yes because you didn't want to seem selfish. The one who dimmed your light because someone once called you too much.

Let yourself mourn.
That mask had a job, and it did it well. But now it's outlived its usefulness.

What Surfaces in the Silence

Here's the wild, beautiful, truth-soaked secret:
The silence after the applause is where you meet your
real self.

At first, it's awkward as hell. You'll be tempted to run
back to the safety of applause, to over-explain, to
apologize for your boundaries, to "fix" everyone's
discomfort.
Don't.

Sit in the quiet.
Let yourself feel the ache of not being needed.
It's the withdrawal before the awakening.

Because in that space, something miraculous
happens:
You start to hear your own voice.

You start to notice your own desires.
You get curious about what you want, what you feel,
what you value—without the noise of everyone else's
expectations.

This is the beginning of authenticity.

And yes, it's scary.

But it's also the birthplace of true belonging.

If You're Not Pleasing... Who Are You?

That's the million-dollar question. Most of us have no idea.

- What do you actually want, outside of what makes others happy?
- What pisses you off, even if it's "inconvenient"?
- What would you do with your time, your body, your life, if no one was watching?

Maybe you don't know. That's okay. Most people-pleasers don't.

That's why the work of becoming your real self can feel so daunting.

It's not just about setting boundaries or saying no—it's about building an identity from the inside out.

It's about becoming someone who can survive the silence.

Someone who can disappoint people and keep breathing.

Someone who can be misunderstood and not over-explain themselves into a coma.

It's about trusting that you are worthy, even without applause.

Reflection Break:

The Real You, Unmasked

Take a moment and let these prompts land:

1. What parts of myself have I edited or hidden to earn approval?
2. What fears come up when I imagine being fully seen without softening the edges?
3. Who would I be if I trusted I was loveable, even when I'm not pleasing?
4. What would I do differently this week if I wasn't seeking applause?

Now write yourself a note:
"I don't need to be impressive to be worthy.
I don't need to be easy to be loved.
I am willing to let go of the performance and let myself be fully known."

Mini Detox Practice: Let Silence Be Enough

This week, when you make a decision, decline something, or express a boundary—resist the urge to over-explain.

Let it land.
Let there be space.
Let there be no applause.

It will feel awkward. You'll itch to fill the silence. But I promise—on the other side of that silence is self-respect. And it's worth more than any fleeting praise.

The Applause Is Addictive. But Peace? Peace Is Sustainable.

You are not who you had to become to feel safe.
You are who you are beneath the noise—a self you may not have met yet, but who has been waiting, patient and whole, for you to come home.

Your worth is not a performance.
Your value is not a popularity contest.

Your legacy will not be the sum of your people-pleasing.

Looking Forward

Next, we'll explore how to stop outsourcing your worth to praise, productivity, and proving. We'll talk about the "inner gold star collector" and the practical, nervous-system-level work of learning to affirm yourself.

Because being loved by the world is wonderful. But being at home in yourself? That's the real revolution.

✦Chapter 5✦

The Inner Gold Star Collector

How to Stop Outsourcing Your Worth to Praise, Productivity, and Proving

The Gold Star Hustle: Why We're All Secretly Keeping Score

Let's tell the truth: most of us have a little gold star collector living somewhere in our heads. They might wear a power suit, a sparkly tutu, or yoga pants—but their job is always the same: keep a tally of every time you earn a compliment, a like, a "thank you," or a "wow, you're amazing."

Every time you:

- Say yes when you mean maybe (or no)
- Over-deliver on a project, even though you're bone-tired
- Hold your tongue to keep the peace
- Stay late, over-function, or come through in a crisis

...your inner collector gleefully slaps a gold star on your invisible chart.

And the world *loves* you for it. You're responsible. You're humble. You're "the rock." You're the one who never drops the ball.

But here's what nobody tells you about collecting gold stars:

It never ends. The chart is never full. The finish line always moves.

You're always one slip away from feeling not enough again.
The satisfaction is fleeting. The hustle is endless.
And eventually, your self-worth is built entirely on external measurement—even as you feel like a ghost inside your own life.

Why Your Brain Loves the Gold Star Game

Ready for a little brain science? When you receive praise, recognition, or even a subtle nod of approval, your brain lights up with dopamine—the same feel-good chemical released when you eat chocolate, win a prize, or get a flurry of likes on your best post.

It feels amazing.
But dopamine is a fickle friend. The more you get, the more you crave.
The high doesn't last. And suddenly, you need a bigger hit—a bigger win, a newer achievement, a fresh round of applause.

So you start chasing:

- More productivity
- More perfection
- More "above and beyond"
- More proof that you're okay

This is how over-achievers, perfectionists, and chronic givers are made. You're not just working for joy or meaning—you're hustling for your next validation fix.

And the more you rely on praise to feel okay, the more intolerant you become of feedback, silence, or even neutrality. Anything less than glowing approval? Feels like failure.

The Proving Loop: How Achievement Becomes Addiction

Let's break down how this cycle keeps you stuck:

1. **You do something exceptional** (or just overextend yourself trying).
2. **You get recognized**. It feels good—for a heartbeat.
3. **The buzz wears off.** You wonder if it was enough, or just luck.
4. **You set the bar higher** for next time—"I'll really impress them now."
5. **You burn yourself out** trying to meet the new standard.
6. **Maybe you get more gold stars—maybe not.**
7. **Repeat.**

You become a master at impressing people—and a stranger to your own needs.

You don't rest. You don't pause.

You don't feel safe unless you're performing.

And here's the wild part:

You can look confident.

You can look successful.

But inside, you're exhausted—and still suspicious you might not be enough.

When "Enough" Is Always Moving

Let's talk about the moving target of "enoughness." If you grew up being rewarded for achievement, helpfulness, or emotional labor, your brain fused worthiness with performance. You don't just *like* praise—you *need* it, because it's the only way you know you're okay.

But the bar always moves:

- You get praised for your grades, so you push for better.
- You're the reliable friend, so you take on more.
- You keep the peace, so you start swallowing your truth by default.

And every time you level up, the standard resets. Your baseline becomes "exceptional," and anything less feels like a failure.

This is why so many high achievers are secretly anxious or depressed. The world sees their trophies; they see only the dust and the missed marks.

Gold Stars as Currency: The Emotional Economy of Proving

Here's the underbelly: In the gold star economy, everything is a transaction.

- You give time, energy, perfectionism, emotional labor.
- You get (hopefully) praise, safety, belonging, or a fleeting sense of being "good."

But the more you give, the less it's worth. People come to expect your best as the bare minimum. Your effort is no longer special. Your "above and beyond" becomes invisible—until you stop, and suddenly you're "letting people down."

It's not generosity. It's a treadmill.

The Crash That Always Comes

You keep hustling until one of two things happens:

1. **You burn out.** The gold stars stop feeling good. The applause rings hollow. You're exhausted, resentful, and secretly angry that nobody sees how hard you're trying.
2. **You mess up.** You fail, disappoint, or just can't keep up. Suddenly, the entire house of cards collapses, and you feel like you're not just failing at something—you're failing at being enough.

That's when you realize:
You've been building your worth on applause instead of anchoring it within.

That realization? As heartbreaking as it is... is your turning point.

What Happens When the Stars Don't Come

Let's get even more real. Sometimes, you do everything "right" and still don't get the love or recognition you crave. Maybe the promotion goes to someone else. Maybe your efforts are taken for granted. Maybe you hit the wall of someone else's indifference or criticism.

And because your worth was built on external metrics, you feel like you disappear.
You start to panic.
You scramble to prove, explain, fix, or outdo yourself.

Or you collapse, numb out, and wonder if you'll ever be "enough" for anyone—including yourself.

The Path to Self-Affirmation: Dismantling the Inner Scorekeeper

Here's the truth bomb: No amount of gold stars from the outside will ever fill the place inside you that's still waiting for your own approval.

If you want real, sustainable self-worth, you have to become your own source of affirmation.
You have to build internal metrics for enoughness— ones that don't depend on applause, likes, or being the hero.

This isn't easy.

But it is possible.

And it's the only way off the treadmill.

Practical Rituals for Breaking the Gold Star Habit

1. Spot Your Inner Collector

Start noticing when your worth spikes or crashes based on feedback, likes, or recognition.
Ask:

- Am I doing this for joy, or for approval?
- What would I do differently if nobody knew or cared?

2. Celebrate Yourself—On Purpose

Every day, write down one thing you're proud of that nobody else saw or rewarded.
Did you rest when you wanted to work?
Say no when you wanted to say yes?
Hold a boundary?
That's a gold star from *you*.

3. Unplug from External Metrics

For one week, try not checking the likes, the stats, the
comments, or the "did they notice?"
Do your work, your art, your life—for the experience,
not the applause.
See what rises.

4. Name Your Enoughness

Each morning, try this mantra:
"I am enough, even when nobody notices.
I am worthy, even when I'm not exceptional.
I do not have to perform to belong."

5. Let Others Disappoint You

This is scary, but vital. Let people miss your efforts.
Let them take you for granted—just for a moment.
Notice that, even when the stars don't come, you still
exist. You still matter.

Reflection Break:

Drop the Scorecard

- In what areas of my life do I feel the constant need to "prove" myself?
- What gold stars am I chasing that no longer bring me joy—but still hold power over my choices?
- What would happen if I did less and trusted that I'm still worthy?
- Who might be disappointed if I stopped performing—and who might be relieved?

Write this somewhere visible:

"I am not a task. I am not a brand. I am not here to impress. I am here to live."

Mini Detox Mission: Do Something Unimpressive (On Purpose)

This week, pick one thing you normally do for praise—and don't do it. Or do it quietly. Or do it badly.

- Let someone else take credit.
- Skip the unnecessary perfection.
- Say "I'm actually not available to help with that."
- Share something unfinished or messy.

- Wear the outfit you love but feel judged in.

And then—don't explain. Don't justify. Just let yourself be... human.

Gold Stars Aren't Bad—But You Deserve More

Let's be clear: External recognition is lovely. We all need some of it. But when your worth depends on it, you're forever stuck on the hamster wheel.

You get to rest. You get to be messy. You get to be enough without earning it.

You are already worthy of love that doesn't require you to shine for it.

Looking Forward

In the next chapter, we'll talk about boundaries—the art of saying no without an apology tour, and learning to disappoint others without betraying yourself. Because the next level of self-loyalty isn't just internal; it's how you show up in the world, even when it ruffles a few feathers.

The Approval Detox

You're not here to collect stars.
You're here to be a constellation.

✦Chapter 6✦

The Hidden Payoff

Why We Keep Pleasing (and What It's Really Costing Us)

The Secret Reward Underneath the Exhaustion

Let's call it what it is: people-pleasing *works*—until it doesn't.

It keeps the peace. It keeps relationships smooth. It keeps you safe (or at least, it feels that way). And deep down, even while you're rolling your eyes at your own inability to say no, a part of you is quietly whispering, *"But this is how I stay loved."*

That whisper? That's the hidden payoff.

Nobody talks about it because it feels shameful to admit—because who wants to say out loud, *"I trade pieces of myself for a sense of control"?* But that's exactly what's happening under the surface.

You're not selfless. You're strategic.

And your strategy makes sense. It's ancient. It's brilliant. It's *exhausting*.

Let's peel it back.

Why We Keep Doing What Hurts

Every pattern that sticks around—especially the ones that wreck your peace—exists because somewhere, it *pays off*.

If you didn't get *something* from pleasing, you'd stop. But you do. We all do.

Here's the real talk:

People-pleasing gives you short-term safety, connection, and predictability.

Every time you avoid conflict by smoothing things over, your nervous system exhales in relief. Every time you say yes instead of risking disappointment, you dodge the spike of anxiety that comes with being misunderstood or disliked.

You tell yourself, *"See? Everything's fine. I didn't upset anyone. I'm good."*

Except "fine" is just fear wearing lipstick.

You trade genuine peace for temporary calm. You trade authenticity for the illusion of control.

And that illusion? That's the drug.

The Four Hidden Payoffs of Pleasing

Let's get honest about what we *really* gain when we people-please.

1. **Safety.**
   The first and deepest payoff is feeling safe. Your nervous system learned that people are less likely to hurt, abandon, or reject you when you're agreeable. "Keep them happy, keep me safe." That belief still drives the bus, even if you know better now.

2. **Control.**
   This one stings. People-pleasing can look submissive, but it's secretly controlling. By managing others' emotions—anticipating, fixing, softening—you control the chaos. It's not about manipulation. It's about survival. But make no mistake: it keeps you busy running

everyone else's weather system instead of tending your own.

3. **Identity.**

   Being the peacemaker, the helper, the "easy one" gives you a role—a reason to exist. It's the story of who you are. If you've built your whole sense of worth on being the reliable one, what happens when you stop? The payoff of belonging through usefulness is powerful.

4. **Avoidance of Grief.**

   Maybe the most hidden one of all: if you stop pleasing, you'd have to face the grief of what you lost along the way—your time, your truth, maybe your childhood safety. Pleasing keeps you too busy to notice the ache. It numbs with productivity.

Each payoff is a life raft that once kept you from drowning. But you're not in that same ocean anymore.

You don't need the life raft—but you're still clinging to it out of habit.

The True Cost: What the Payoff Steals

Every short-term payoff carries a long-term tax.

Let's tally it.

- **Safety's cost:** perpetual anxiety. You stay hyper-alert, managing everyone's comfort, but you never actually feel safe—because your safety depends on everyone else's approval.
- **Control's cost:** exhaustion. You become the world's emotional janitor, cleaning up everyone's messes.
- **Identity's cost:** invisibility. You mistake being needed for being known.
- **Avoidance's cost:** numbing. You forget what joy even feels like because you've spent so long avoiding discomfort.

The receipts don't lie.

You're overdrawn in self-trust.
You're bankrupt in joy.
You're rich in burnout.

And all that to feel "okay" for what—ten minutes?

Let's stop pretending this trade is fair.

The Relationship Illusion

Here's another sneaky payoff: you think pleasing earns love. But what it mostly earns is *dependence*.

When you please, people don't love *you*—they love what you do for them. They love the ease, the yeses, the predictability. They love the version of you that keeps their life tidy.

But the real you—the one with boundaries, needs, or opinions—doesn't get to show up.

That's the heartbreak every recovering people-pleaser faces: realizing you've built relationships around the mask, not the soul underneath it.

And when you start peeling back the performance, some of those relationships crack. That's not failure— that's alignment.

If someone only loves you when you disappear, their love isn't love. It's maintenance.

The Biology of the Payoff

Here's where science backs the soul work:

Every time you please and avoid discomfort, your brain rewards you with a hit of dopamine and oxytocin—bonding chemicals. You feel safe and connected, even if it's fake peace.

But when you risk conflict (say, by saying no), your brain triggers cortisol—the stress hormone. It screams *danger!* Even if you're just asserting a boundary.

So your body literally believes that being honest = threat, and people-pleasing = safety.

You're not crazy for choosing the "safe" route. You're chemically conditioned to do it.

But now you can recondition yourself—one honest "no" at a time.

The Reckoning: Choosing Depth Over Comfort

The hidden payoff loses power the second you expose it.

Once you name it, you have a choice:
Will you keep settling for safety on someone else's

terms, or will you risk discomfort for the freedom of being real?

Here's the paradox: what feels unsafe at first—saying no, disappointing someone, dropping the mask—is the only true path to lasting safety.

Real peace comes from alignment, not approval.

Because the rush of being liked can't compare to the quiet relief of being authentic.

Reflection Break:

Expose the Payoff

1. What discomfort does people-pleasing help me avoid? (Conflict? Rejection? Guilt? Chaos?)
2. What do I *gain* from over-giving or over-achieving? Name the specific reward.
3. What does it cost me—emotionally, physically, spiritually—to keep paying for that reward?
4. Who might I become if I stopped earning safety through compliance?

Write it, don't judge it. Awareness is detox.

Mini Detox Mission: Trade the Shortcut for the Soul Work

This week, every time you catch yourself pleasing, pause and name the payoff:

- "I'm doing this because I want to be liked."
- "I'm doing this because it makes me feel in control."
- "I'm doing this because I don't want to feel guilty."

Then ask yourself: *Is this payoff worth the price?*

Just asking that question interrupts the trance. It loosens the grip.

If you're brave, take it further: say no, disappoint gently, or let silence do the work.
Then watch what happens. You'll survive. In fact, you'll expand.

Closing Truths

You don't owe anyone your constant comfort-crafting. You don't have to earn your belonging by disappearing.

You don't have to call your self-abandonment "kindness."

The hidden payoff kept you safe once.
Now it's keeping you stuck.

Trade false safety for real peace.
Trade temporary control for embodied freedom.
Trade gold stars for grounded truth.

You are allowed to stop managing the room.
You are allowed to let discomfort exist.
You are allowed to choose yourself without apology.

Real love—the kind that sticks—doesn't require your performance.
It invites your presence.

And that? That's the only payoff worth keeping.

Part II: Disrupting the Pattern

✦Chapter 7✦

The Approval Hangover

Why Praise Never Feels Like Enough—And How to Detox From the Crash

The High and the Hollow

You know that feeling: You get the compliment, the like, the "You did so much for us!" The email chimes with thanks, the group chat blows up with applause, your boss or your lover or your best friend gives you that look that says, "You're my hero."

And for a moment—maybe five minutes, maybe a whole day—you're floating. Shoulders back, chin up, heart light. You did it. You're seen. You're wanted. You're safe.

But then...

It fades.
The texts stop.
The likes slow down.
The high drains away, and what's left is a hollow ache.

Maybe a little shame, maybe a little emptiness, maybe a new, sharper edge to your old hunger.

You start wondering:
Did I really deserve it?
Will it last?
Do they mean it?
What if I can't keep it up next time?

And sometimes, you crash even harder than before.

Welcome to the **approval hangover**—that emotional whiplash when praise feels good, but never good enough.

Why Praise Feels Like Oxygen—And Why It's Not

Let's be clear: There's nothing wrong with wanting to be appreciated, recognized, or loved. Humans are wired for connection, and a little affirmation goes a long way. But when your nervous system *needs* praise to feel okay, it isn't just a treat—it's a drug.

You start to live for the next fix:

- The next "thank you"
- The next gold star at work
- The next "wow, you're amazing"
- The next "I couldn't do this without you"

And every time you get it, you get a dopamine rush. You feel alive. But the effect is temporary, and when it fades, you're left... wanting.

It's not because you're ungrateful.
It's because your system was trained to survive on external validation.
And like all quick highs, the comedown is brutal.

The Psychology of Praise Resistance

Here's the part most people-pleasers never say out loud: Sometimes, even when you receive praise, you can't actually take it in. Maybe you deflect compliments, downplay your achievements, or instantly credit someone else.

Why? Because somewhere inside, you're braced for the "but."

- "I love you, but..."

- "You're great, but could you just..."
- "That was amazing, but next time..."

So, when someone affirms you, your body flinches. You might even feel suspicious or undeserving, waiting for the other shoe to drop.

This is praise resistance. It's your nervous system not trusting that goodness will last—or that you're allowed to rest in it.

Why the Crash Feels So Personal

When the high of approval wears off, you're not just disappointed. You might feel embarrassed, empty, or even angry at yourself for wanting more.

You might spiral into self-doubt:

- "Am I that needy?"
- "Why can't I just be satisfied?"
- "Is something wrong with me?"

But here's the truth: There's nothing wrong with you. You're just living in a system—internal and external— that conditions you to chase validation and then punishes you for needing it.

It's a setup.

And the hangover is proof.

The Real Cost of Living for Praise

Let's get honest about what this cycle actually steals from you:

- **Joy:** You can't fully celebrate your wins, because you're already bracing for the crash.
- **Rest:** You can't relax unless you're being noticed, wanted, or needed.
- **Self-trust:** You doubt your own value unless someone's stamping it with a compliment.
- **Presence:** You're always scanning for feedback, missing the actual experience of your life.
- **Satisfaction:** Nothing ever lands deep enough, so you're always hustling for the next fix.

You become dependent on praise, but allergic to actually receiving it.

And the hollowness grows.

Healing the Hangover: Learning to Receive

Here's the wild idea: What if you didn't have to earn every kind word?
What if you were already worthy—before the applause, before the achievement, before the A+?

Learning to receive is the antidote to the approval hangover.

- When someone compliments you, say, "Thank you."
  (Full stop. No "but…", no "It was nothing.")
- When you succeed at something, pause and let yourself feel proud.
  (No minimizing, no self-deprecation.)
- When love shows up, don't distract or deflect. Let it touch you—even if it feels awkward.

Receiving is vulnerable. It's intimate. For most people-pleasers, it's terrifying.
But it's also where the healing happens.

Reflection Break:

Unpacking the Hangover

1. When I receive praise or validation, what's my immediate emotional reaction?
2. What scripts or beliefs come up when someone sees or celebrates me?
3. What do I fear will happen if I fully enjoy being appreciated?
4. What's one compliment I deflected recently—and what would it have felt like to receive it?

Now write this truth somewhere visible:
"I don't have to earn every kind word.
I don't have to justify being celebrated.
I don't have to reject what nourishes me.
I am learning to let love land."

Mini Detox Practice: Sit With the Good

This week, choose one moment of appreciation—big or small—and don't brush it off.

- Accept the compliment.
- Re-read the thank-you email.

- Let yourself feel proud of something you did well.
- Share your win without apologizing for it.

Then take a breath and say:
"This belongs to me. And I'm allowed to enjoy it."

That's not ego. That's healing.

What If It Never Feels Like Enough?

Let's be real: There will be days when no amount of praise feels like it fills you up. On those days, don't beat yourself up for being "too needy" or "too sensitive."
Instead, get curious.
Ask: "What am I actually longing for beneath this?"

Often, it's not more praise—it's permission to rest, to be loved as you are, to stop hustling for your own worth.

That permission won't come from the outside.
It starts with you.

Looking Forward

In the next chapter, we'll talk about the "lie of being too much"—how people-pleasers learn to shrink, self-edit, and apologize for their own existence. We'll explore what it means to actually take up space, let yourself be seen, and make room for the fullness of who you are.

The hangover is a sign you're ready for something deeper than applause.
It's a call to belong to yourself.

✦Chapter 8✦

The Lie of Being "Too Much"

How to Stop Shrinking, Start Expanding, and Actually Let Yourself Be Seen

Too Loud, Too Sensitive, Too Intense, Too "You"

If you're a lifelong people-pleaser, you've heard it—maybe not always in words, but in sighs, silences, or the way people look away when your truth gets big. You're "too much."
Too loud. Too emotional. Too direct. Too sensitive. Too needy. Too ambitious. Too opinionated. Too passionate. Too... whatever makes someone else squirm.

Translation?
You're inconvenient. You make people uncomfortable. Please, shrink. Be easier to digest.

And so you learned: dial it down, bite your tongue, water yourself down to a version of you that never asks, never disrupts, never offends.

Let's name it:

This is not humility.

This is self-abandonment in a sugarcoat.

Where the "Too Much" Script Comes From

The "too much" story is rarely handed to you as a single, clear message.

It seeps in through:

- Family systems where emotions were "handled privately," or not at all.
- Classrooms that praised the quiet, compliant, and easy-to-manage.
- Friend groups that rolled their eyes when you got passionate, or changed the subject when you got vulnerable.
- Relationships where your needs were "a lot," your dreams were "unrealistic," or your boundaries were "selfish."
- Cultures, faith traditions, or workplaces that reward sameness, not individuality; silence, not honesty.

Sometimes, it's overt:
"Stop being so dramatic."
"You're so sensitive!"
"Why can't you just be chill?"

More often, it's subtle:
A raised eyebrow, a withheld invitation, a sudden chill in the room.

Over time, you internalize the lesson:
If I shrink, I'll be safe.
If I'm easy, I'll be loved.

But here's the secret nobody tells you:
You cannot make yourself small enough to be truly loved by people who only want the edited version of you.

Shrinking as a Survival Strategy

Let's honor your intelligence: You didn't shrink because you were weak. You shrank because it kept you connected, or at least less at risk.

You learned to:

• Edit your opinions so you don't ruffle feathers.

- Laugh off the jokes that sting.
- Soften your boundaries ("It's fine, really!") to avoid being labeled difficult.
- Say "It's no big deal" when it's absolutely a big deal.
- Become an expert at reading the room, scanning for danger, and adjusting your volume, mood, or truth accordingly.

You became the emotional chameleon, always matching the temperature of the people around you.

But what about your own weather?
What about the wild, vivid, unfiltered you?

The True Cost of Shrinking

Let's get brutally honest:

- **Your relationships become shallow.** No one can love the real you if you never show up unscripted.
- **Your dreams get smaller.** You stop reaching beyond what others can tolerate.
- **You lose your sense of self.** You become easy to like, hard to know—even to yourself.

- **Your body rebels.** Chronic tension, anxiety, exhaustion, and even illness are common for long-term shrinkers.
- **You become resentful.** You keep the peace, but you also keep score.

You may be liked, but you're rarely loved in the way you long for:
Seen, felt, met, chosen—as you are.

The Myth of "Not Enough" vs. "Too Much"

Here's the cosmic joke: The lie of "too much" is just the flip side of the "not enough" story.
You're either too much for some or not enough for others.

But the real truth is this:
You will always be "too much" for people committed to mediocrity, and "not enough" for those who need you to fill their emptiness. Neither of those is your job.

Your job is to be fully, unapologetically yourself, and let the world recalibrate around your wholeness.

What It Actually Means to Take Up Space

Taking up space doesn't mean monopolizing attention, bulldozing others, or being "on" all the time. It means:

- Showing up with your full emotional range: joy, anger, grief, awe.
- Naming your needs, desires, and limits— without apology.
- Laughing loudly, crying openly, loving fiercely.
- Allowing your presence to be felt, not hidden.
- Trusting that your impact is a gift, even if it sometimes makes others uncomfortable.

Taking up space is a reclamation, not a rebellion.

The World Needs Your Fullness

Let's be clear:
The world is not hungry for more agreeable, shrink-to-fit humans.
The world is starving for the wild, honest, inconvenient magic of people who refuse to edit their souls.

Every time you let yourself be seen—messy, passionate, direct, alive—you give permission to everyone else who's been hiding.

Your "too much" is someone else's lifeline.

Micro-Detox Practice: Let Yourself Be Seen

This week, choose one safe-ish context and let your fullness show for real.

- Wear the outfit that feels a little "extra."
- Share the story that's vulnerable, unedited, and real.
- Let yourself cry where you'd normally go numb.
- Say the thing you usually swallow.
- Occupy your space in the room—shoulders back, eye contact, breath deep.

Notice what happens in your body. Name the urge to shrink, but don't obey it.

When the inner critic whispers, "You're too much," answer back:

"No. I'm finally enough. And I'm done apologizing."

Reflection Break:

Reclaiming Your "Too Much"

1. What parts of myself have I been told are "too much" for others to handle?
2. Where in my life do I currently shrink or dilute myself to avoid discomfort?
3. What would it feel like to stop apologizing for being who I am?
4. What do I gain—and what do I lose—by making myself smaller?

Now write this declaration (out loud, if you dare):
"I am not too much.
I am deep, wide, alive, and powerful.
My fullness is not a flaw—it is a force.
And I will no longer apologize for it."

When Others Can't Handle Your Fullness

Let's set the record straight: Some people will fall away when you expand. Some will gossip, withdraw, or try to stuff you back in the box.
This is not a tragedy.
It's a filter.

Your fullness will attract those who are ready for you—and repel those who aren't.

Let it.

Looking Forward

In the next chapter, we'll talk about reparenting the part of you that learned to earn love by shrinking. We'll explore how to give yourself the permission, safety, and sweet celebration you've been craving from the world.

You are not here to be a bite-sized human.
You are here for soul-stretching, joy-expanding, boundary-breaking, full-bodied living.

Let the world adjust.

✦Chapter 9✦

Shadow Work for the Chronic People-Pleaser

Rage, Manipulation, Martyrdom, and the Secret Self Beneath the Smile

The Smile That Hides the Storm

Let's get this out of the way: People-pleasers are not "nice." They're *dangerous*—in the most quietly corrosive way.

Not to others, necessarily—but to themselves.

That smile you plaster on when you're dying inside? That's power turned inward. That's fire bottled up so tight it starts to rot.

Because for years, you've probably been trying to be the light in every room. The peacemaker, the fix-it fairy, the "no worries, I've got it" friend.

But every persona has a shadow.

And the shadow of "nice" isn't sweetness.

It's resentment.

It's control.

It's quiet, festering rage.

You've spent years polishing your halo—and now, it's time to look at the horns underneath.

Not because you're bad. But because you're *whole*.

What Is Shadow Work, Really?

Let's de-mystify this. Shadow work isn't witchcraft, sin-hunting, or a moral detox. It's the sacred practice of facing the parts of yourself you've shoved in the basement because they didn't fit the good-person costume.

Your shadow is the collection of traits, feelings, and impulses you learned were "unacceptable." It's your repressed anger. Your envy. Your ego. Your desire. Your need to control. Your craving to be adored.

And it's not evil—it's *information*.

The shadow always tells the truth about what you've been suppressing. If ignored, it leaks out sideways—in sarcasm, martyrdom, guilt trips, or burnout disguised as generosity.

Shadow work is how your buried self finally gets a voice.

It's not about fixing what's wrong with you.
It's about meeting what's real in you—with honesty, not judgment.

The Polite Mask and Its Rebellions

Let's tell the truth: chronic niceness is rebellion disguised as compliance.

You might follow every rule, meet every expectation, and smile through every discomfort—but beneath that polished exterior, a storm is brewing.

Because the self can only stay exiled for so long before it finds sneaky ways to speak.

Ever been "helpful" in a way that secretly punished the person you were helping?
Ever agreed to something with a smile but then quietly resented every minute of it?

Ever withdrawn affection to make a point—while still insisting, *"I'm fine, really"*?

That's your shadow, tapping the mic.

It's the part of you sick of playing saint.

The part that's done performing nice.

The part that's demanding to be real.

The Hidden Rage Beneath "I'm Fine"

Let's talk about rage—the emotion people-pleasers fear most.

Rage is not the enemy. It's a messenger.

Anger shows up when a boundary's been crossed, when a truth has been ignored, when a part of you is screaming, *"I'm done being polite about this."*

You've probably been swallowing your anger since you were old enough to notice that other people's comfort mattered more than your truth. So now, anger terrifies you—not because you don't feel it, but because it feels uncontrollable.

So you shove it down. You smile instead.
You "understand." You "don't want to make a big deal."

But here's the catch: swallowed rage doesn't disappear.
It mutates.

It becomes resentment.
It becomes exhaustion.
It becomes a passive-aggressive agreement followed by emotional withdrawal.

And here's the shadow twist—when you suppress your fire long enough, it starts burning you instead of lighting the way.

The Manipulative Pleaser

This one's tough to admit. Because when you've built your identity around being "nice," the last thing you want to see is how manipulative kindness can be.

But here it is: people-pleasing *is* a form of manipulation.

That's not a moral judgment—it's a nervous-system strategy.

When you alter your behavior to control someone's reaction—to avoid rejection, anger, or disapproval—you're not just being considerate. You're trying to *manage* their emotional landscape.

And that's manipulation in its gentlest disguise.

You say yes to keep them happy (so you feel safe).
You apologize to calm their ego (so you don't have to face conflict).
You give endlessly (so nobody ever leaves).

You're not evil. You're strategic. You're trying to survive.

But survival mode isn't intimacy.
Manipulation might keep the peace—but it kills authenticity.

The Martyr's Crown

Raise your hand if you've ever been the one holding it all together while whispering, *"It's fine, I've got it,"* but secretly dying inside.

The Approval Detox

Welcome to the Martyr Olympics.

The medal? Chronic resentment disguised as virtue.

Martyrdom is people-pleasing evolved into sainthood.
It's the performance of perpetual self-sacrifice. It
looks noble. It earns praise. It feels morally superior.

But here's the twisted truth: martyrdom lets you feel
powerful *without* asking for what you actually need.

Instead of saying, "I'm hurt," you over-give until they
feel guilty.
Instead of saying, "I need help," you power through
until you collapse.
Instead of setting boundaries, you weaponize
exhaustion.

It's control through suffering—and you learned it from
generations of good humans who survived by
disappearing.

You don't have to repeat the pattern.

Meeting the Secret Self

Beneath the anger, control, and martyrdom lives the part of you that never got to be honest. The Secret Self.

They're messy, emotional, opinionated, needy, sensual, selfish, ambitious—all the things you were told not to be.

But this self isn't "bad." They're human. They're *you*.

Your shadow isn't trying to destroy your light—it's trying to make it honest. Because real light doesn't come from denying your dark; it comes from integrating it.

Every piece you disown finds another way to demand attention. But when you turn toward it, when you say, *"I see you, and you get to exist,"* something shifts.

You relax.
You stop performing.
You become someone whole, not just someone good.

The Shadow Alchemy Process

Working with your shadow isn't about unleashing chaos; it's about cultivating wholeness.

Here's how to start:

1. **Notice the triggers.**
   When you catch yourself judging someone for being selfish, dramatic, lazy, or demanding—pause. That's often your shadow pointing at its reflection.

2. **Name what's underneath.**
   Ask, "What part of me wants to do that but doesn't feel allowed to?"

3. **Claim safe expression.**
   - Rage? Move it. Punch a pillow. Write an unsent letter.
   - Resentment? Speak the truth, calmly.
   - Desire? Admit it to yourself, even if you don't act on it yet.

4. **Use compassion, not condemnation.**
   The goal isn't to scold your shadow—it's to integrate it. The more you judge it, the louder it gets.

5. **Rewrite the story.**

   Instead of "I'm manipulative," try "I learned to influence others to feel safe, and I'm learning better ways to meet that need."

You're not broken. You're brilliant.
You were surviving with the tools you had.
Now, you're evolving.

Reflection Break:

Meeting the Self in the Mirror

1. What emotions or traits do I judge most harshly in myself—or others?
2. Where do I secretly crave control, even when I pretend it's selflessness?
3. What's a situation where my "niceness" was really resentment in disguise?
4. What would it feel like to let my anger, desire, or truth exist without an apology?

Now write this truth somewhere visible:

"My shadow is not my enemy.
It is the part of me that remembers what I buried to stay loved."

Micro-Detox Mission: Make Friends With Your Fire

This week, do something radical: give your shadow airtime.

- Admit an inconvenient truth—to yourself or someone safe.
- Let yourself say, "I'm angry," without sugarcoating.
- Stop over-giving where you secretly resent.
- Do something selfish, just to see that the world doesn't end.

When the guilt rushes in, place a hand on your heart and say:
"I'm allowed to be whole. I don't have to be holy to be worthy."

That's shadow integration. It's not pretty—but it's liberation.

The Sacred Rebellion of Wholeness

Shadow work is not an exorcism of your dark—it's a reunion of what's real.

When you stop banishing your rage, you stop pretending peace.
When you stop disowning your desire, you stop calling it weakness.
When you stop performing selflessness, you start living self-loyalty.

This is what integrity actually means: integrating all your parts—rage and tenderness, compassion and boundaries, love and truth.

You don't heal by becoming nicer.
You heal by becoming *honest*.

And from that honesty, love has room to be real.

✦Chapter 10✦

Saying No Without Explaining Yourself to Death

Boundaries as a Radical Act of Self-Trust (and Not an Apology Tour)

The Sacred, Scary, Two-Letter Word

Let's get one thing straight: "No" is not a dirty word. But if you're a recovering people-pleaser, it sure feels like one.

You've probably been there—heart pounding, stomach twisting, rehearsing your refusal like you're prepping for a Supreme Court hearing. You know you have to say no. But instead of just saying it, you launch into a full-blown TED Talk of apologies, disclaimers, backstory, and preemptive guilt.

"Sorry, I wish I could, but I just have so much going on, and maybe next week, and I feel terrible and..."

Sound familiar?

This is the apology tour. It's exhausting, it's unnecessary, and it's a dead giveaway that you're still trying to buy approval with your boundaries.

But here's the truth bomb:
Saying no is not a rejection of others. It's a radical return to yourself.

Why Is Saying No So Hard?

Let's unmask the real reason. For most of us, saying no wasn't just discouraged—it was dangerous. Maybe you got shamed, guilted, ignored, or even punished for having boundaries as a kid. Maybe you learned early that pleasing equals safety, and no equals "selfish," "difficult," or "ungrateful."

Add a dash of cultural pressure—be agreeable, be helpful, never rock the boat—and you've got a recipe for chronic over-accommodation.

Your nervous system now treats "no" as a threat. Saying it feels like standing on the edge of a social cliff.
Will they hate me?

Will I lose my place?
Will I be left out?

This is not a personal defect—it's survival programming. But it's time to update your operating system.

The Hidden Cost of Over-Explaining

Every time you explain your no to death, you:

- Signal that your boundaries are negotiable
- Invite debate, persuasion, or guilt-tripping
- Undercut your own authority
- Exhaust yourself with unnecessary emotional labor

You end up feeling resentful, depleted, and bewildered about why nobody takes your "no" seriously.

And here's the kicker:
The people who respect boundaries don't need an explanation.
The people who don't will never find your reason "good enough."

The Clean "No" (and Why It's Spiritual, Sexy, and Sovereign)

A clean no is a complete sentence. It's not padded with apology, justification, or shame.

Here's what a clean no sounds like:

- "No, thank you."
- "That's not going to work for me."
- "I'm not available for that."
- "I appreciate the ask, but I'll pass."
- "No."

No fluff. No fake apologies. Just truth, delivered with respect.

Why is this spiritual? Because it's a declaration that you trust yourself.
Why is it sexy? Because nothing is more attractive than someone who knows and honors their own limits.
Why is it sovereign? Because it's you, holding your own ground—not waiting for permission.

Scripts for Saying No (Without the TED Talk)

Let's make this practical. Here are some sassy, solid, and succinct scripts to keep in your back pocket:

- **Work:** "Thanks for thinking of me, but I can't take that on right now."
- **Family:** "No, I'm not available this weekend."
- **Friends:** "I'd love to see you, but tonight isn't good for me."
- **Volunteering:** "I'm not able to help out this time. Hope it goes well!"
- **Emotional labor:** "I'm not in a place to talk about this right now. Can we check in another time?"

And if someone pushes?

Just repeat.

"No, that doesn't work for me."

(Repeat as needed.)

The Nervous System Freakout: How to Survive the Guilt Storm

Let's not sugarcoat it: The first time you offer a clean no, your body will revolt.
You'll feel guilty. You'll want to explain. You'll panic at the silence.

This is your nervous system detoxing from years of over-accommodation.
It's not a sign you're doing it wrong.
It's a sign you're finally doing it right.

Try this:

- Place a hand on your heart.
- Take a slow, steady breath.
- Whisper: "My needs matter. I'm allowed to take up space. I trust myself to survive this discomfort."

Let the guilt, the awkwardness, the urge to fix—move through you.
Don't let it run the show.

Reflection Break:

Your Relationship With "No"

- What do I fear people will think of me if I say no without an explanation?
- Where in my life am I saying yes when I actually mean no?
- Who benefits from me having weak boundaries—and who would I become if I stopped performing?
- What would change in my body, energy, and spirit if I stopped apologizing for honoring my limits?

Write your truth. Even if it stings.

Micro-Detox Mission: The One-Line "No"

This week, choose one small thing to decline with a single sentence.

Not:

"Oh, I wish I could, but honestly, I've just had the busiest week and I feel terrible but I hope it's okay and maybe next time and..."

Instead:

"Thanks for thinking of me—I won't be able to this time."

Then stop.
Don't fill the silence. Don't explain.
Let the discomfort rise and pass.
That's the recalibration.

When the World Pushes Back

Here's the reality check:
Some people will be surprised. Some will push back.
Some will sulk, guilt-trip, or try to argue.

This is not evidence you're wrong.
It's evidence you're disrupting an old contract.

Stay the course.
The people who belong in your life will adapt.

The ones who don't? That's information, not a disaster.

No Is a Complete Sentence (and a Love Letter to Yourself)

Every time you say no, you say yes to something deeper:

- Your rest
- Your integrity
- Your self-respect
- Your joy
- Your real "yes"

Boundaries aren't rejection.
They're invitations—to more honest, mutual, and sustainable relationships.

You do not have to explain your existence.
You do not have to apologize for taking up space.

Your "no" is sacred.
Your "yes" is a gift.

Looking Forward

Next, we'll go deeper into what happens after you set a boundary—the "approval hangover." We'll talk about why praise and validation never quite fill you up, and how to start receiving from a place of wholeness, not hunger.

You're not here to be digestible, compliant, or convenient.
You're here to be fully alive.

✦Chapter 11✦

The Energetics of Approval-Seeking

How Your Vibe Attracts Takers, Drama, and "Coincidences" (and What to Do Instead)

The Frequency of Desperation

Let's talk energy—not in the fluffy, incense-only way, but in the nervous-system-meets-physics way.

Everything you do—your tone, body tension, breath, even your texts—broadcasts a signal. And people pick up on that signal long before words arrive.

Approval-seekers run on a very specific energetic frequency: *Please like me, so I can relax.*

It's subtle. You call it friendliness. Generosity. Empathy. But underneath it hums an unspoken plea: *"I'll over-give, over-perform, over-explain—just don't disconnect from me."*

Guess who hears that broadcast loudest?
Takers. Drainers. Unavailable partners. Authority figures who thrive on adoration.

They feel your adaptability and think: *Ah, here's someone who will bend.*

That's not your fault—it's your vibration handing out free passes to people who sense opportunity.

The good news? You can retune.

The Law of Emotional Magnetism

You don't attract what you *deserve*—you attract what you *believe you need to survive.*

If your nervous system learned that safety = harmony, then your body unconsciously searches for dynamics that keep you working for harmony. You'll magnetize relationships that recreate the proof:
"I have to keep earning peace."

It's not cosmic punishment. It's pattern recognition.

Your vibe tells the room how to treat you.
It says:

- "I'll orient toward your needs first."
- "My boundaries are flexible; just smile at me."
- "If you withdraw affection, I'll chase to fix it."

That's the *energetic contract* of approval-seeking. And until you rewrite it, you'll keep meeting different versions of the same taker, wrapped in new clothing.

Nervous Systems Talk to Each Other

Science time.

When two humans interact, their nervous systems sync—heart rate, tone, micro-expressions, even breathing patterns. It's called **co-regulation**.

People with strong boundaries radiate calm steadiness; others adjust to match.
People with anxious approval energy radiate hyper-vigilance; others either exploit it or get drained by it.

Your vibe literally shifts the chemical atmosphere between you and others.

Approval energy feels like static: fast, forward-leaning, eager. It makes your speech rush, your breath shallow, your body tilt slightly toward whoever you're trying to please.

Embodied self-trust feels like gravity: slower, grounded, eyes steady, no reach. It says, *"I'm sovereign."* People feel that difference even if they can't name it.

The Drama Feedback Loop

Ever notice how the more you try to keep everything smooth, the more chaos you attract?

That's because ungrounded "fixer energy" invites drama. The moment you tune your nervous system toward *others' comfort*, you unconsciously step into their storm to calm it—then wonder why your life feels like a reality-show marathon.

Takers love this loop. Drama feeds them attention, and your urge to restore balance feeds them energy. You become their emotional power source—mistaking exhaustion for love.

Until you stop broadcasting *availability for chaos.*

That moment you stop rescuing, you'll watch half your stress evaporate overnight.

Not because the world got kinder.

Because your frequency stopped inviting storms.

The Hidden Currency of "Good Vibes"

Here's another trap: the people-pleaser version of spirituality.

You tell yourself you must "stay positive," "raise your vibration," or "manifest from love." But secretly, that's energetic code for "don't upset anyone."

Positivity becomes performance. Your light gets brittle.

Authentic high frequency doesn't mean relentless cheer—it means coherence: your insides and outsides match.

False "good vibes" repel real intimacy. Coherent energy magnetizes truth.

You can't fake aligned vibration. You have to *feel what you feel* so your system can regulate back to center.

Retuning the Field: Practical Energy Work

1. **Anchor before connection.**
    Before entering a conversation, meeting, or text thread, take one breath and drop into your body. Notice your feet, your seat, your spine. Ask, "Am I leaning toward approval or resting in authenticity?"

2. **Contain your field.**
    Visualize your energy staying within your own skin—not leaking outward to scan or please. This isn't walls; it's sovereignty.

3. **Regulate through exhale.**
    Approval energy rides on shallow inhale. Lengthen your exhale—literally tell your nervous system, "We're safe. We don't have to earn air."

4. **Speak slower than your fear.**
    Pace sets the tone. When you slow down, you lead energetically instead of chasing harmony.

5. **Clean energetic tabs.**
    After intense interactions, imagine unplugging invisible cords from everyone you tried to

impress or soothe. Breathe. Return that energy home.

This isn't "woo." It's biology meeting intention.

The Shift: From Pleasing Vibe to Presence Vibe

Let's map the difference:

Old Frequency	New Frequency
"Do they like me?"	"Do I respect my own energy here?"
Forward-leaning, performative	Upright, relaxed, witnessing
Hyper-tuned to others' tone	Tuned to self-regulation
Anxiety disguised as warmth	Calm that invites honesty
Magnetic to takers	Magnetic to equals

Presence doesn't chase. Presence *invites*.
And that changes everything.

When the Vibe Changes, So Do the Characters

Here's what shocks most recovering pleasers: when you shift your energetic stance, people behave differently—or disappear.

- Some folks suddenly seem colder. That's because your absence of chase removes their supply.
- Some relationships feel awkward. That's recalibration; your system no longer fits their pattern.
- Some new people feel peaceful from day one. That's resonance.

It's not magic; it's mechanics. You're no longer transmitting the frequency of scarcity, so scarcity stops responding.

Reflection Break:

Energetic Autopsy

1. What kinds of people or situations repeatedly drain me?

2. Before those interactions, what emotion usually lives in my body—anxiety, anticipation, guilt?

3. How might that signal invite the very dynamic I dislike?

4. What would "energetic neutrality" feel like in my body right now?

5. Who am I when I'm not performing peace?

Now write this reminder somewhere visible:

"My energy teaches others how to meet me.
I no longer broadcast desperation.
I transmit presence."

Micro-Detox Practice: Embody the Unbothered Frequency

Every day this week, pick one small situation where you'd normally hustle for approval—a text reply, a meeting, a social post—and try this experiment:

- Drop your shoulders.
- Lengthen your exhale.
- Ask, *"Am I trying to be impressive or honest?"*
- Choose honesty. Then do less.

Notice how people respond. Notice, too, how your body exhales when you stop over-sending yourself.

That's not arrogance. That's a balanced signal.

The Quantum Reframe

Here's the spiritual truth in scientific language: energy seeks equilibrium. When you vibrate at self-trust, you naturally repel anything rooted in manipulation.

You don't have to fight for better relationships—you just have to stop radiating "convince me to belong."

Self-respect is a quiet frequency. But it moves mountains.

You can't fake it, but you can cultivate it through consistency.
Every boundary spoken, every pause instead of apology, every breath claimed as yours—it all retunes the field.

And soon, coincidence shifts:
The takers fade.

The peaceful ones appear.
The world matches your new voltage.

Closing Truths

Approval energy says, "See me so I can exist."
Aligned energy says, "I exist, and from that grounding
I choose connection."

One demands audience.
The other radiates reality.

When you stop begging to be read correctly, you start
living clearly.
When your vibe stops asking for validation, you
become magnetic to truth.

You are no longer the frequency of needing.
You're the broadcast of being.

Welcome to energetic maturity.

✦Chapter 12✦

The Quantum No

Becoming Unavailable for Bullsh*t — Energetic Boundaries That Actually Stick

The Art of the Elegant Nope

Congratulations, you're officially done collecting red flags like merit badges.

This is the chapter where we retire the sentence: *"Well, maybe if I just explain myself better..."*

Nope.

The **Quantum No** is not about slamming doors or screaming "boundaries!!" through gritted teeth. It's an energetic stance—a full-body, frequency-level *unavailability* for nonsense.

Think of it as your system's auto-immune upgrade: it recognizes bullsh*t instantly and deletes it before it spreads.

No performance. No debate. No PowerPoint explaining your worth.

Just quiet, sovereign energy that says: *"Not on this frequency, babe."*

When Boundaries Become Biochemistry

Let's get nerdy for a sec. Real boundaries don't start with words; they start with *regulation.*

A dysregulated nervous system can't hold a no—it panics, over-explains, guilt-spirals, and backpedals until "No" becomes "Maybe later."

A regulated body, on the other hand, is the bouncer at the velvet rope of your peace.

So before you text, talk, or declare, breathe. Let your spine remember gravity. Feel that internal yes/no switch toggle on.

That's the frequency of the Quantum No—rooted, relaxed, and non-negotiable.

When your body believes your boundary, everyone else does too.

Approval Detox Aftermath: The Temptation to Relapse

Let's be honest: you'll be tested.

After years of pleasing, your new calm feels suspiciously like rebellion. People from your old timeline will try to re-add you to their drama subscription plan.

You'll get tempting invitations like:

- "Can you just squeeze this in?"
- "Wow, you've changed—you used to be so flexible."
- "You're being cold."

That's breakpoint energy.

Your job: don't audition. Decline *gracefully savage*.

Picture yourself sipping coffee and saying, "You're right...I have changed. I like me better this way."

No tantrum, no essay—just detachment with sparkle.

The Physics of the Quantum No

Energy obeys laws. One is **resonance.**

The more you chase, the more distance you create.
The more you settle, the more chaos you invite.
But the moment you anchor in self-respect, reality
rearranges itself to match.

That's why it's called the *Quantum* No—it doesn't just
stop a behavior; it shifts your probability field.

People who once blurred your boundaries
simply...lose access. The opportunity calls you
dreaded? Canceled. The energy vampire? Blocked by
circumstance, sometimes literally.

Is it magic? Technically, it's coherence. But yeah, it
feels witchy.

Examples of the Quantum No in Action

- **Text Triage:**
  "Thanks for thinking of me. I'm a no for now,

but I hope it goes beautifully!" → Sent, sighed, closed app. No guilt scroll afterward.

- **Meeting Madness:**
  When the boss hints you should "go the extra mile," you smile sweetly and say, "Happy to deliver within my lane." Translation: boundary without burnout.
- **Family Circus:**
  Aunt Linda tries to recruit you into the family drama group chat. You respond with: "I'm sitting this one out—but sending peace to everyone." Poof. Exit stage left.

That's the Quantum No—minimal words, maximal frequency.

The Guilt Ghost

Every recovering pleaser meets the Guilt Ghost—the voice hissing, *"Who do you think you are, saying no?"*

Answer it like this: *"Someone who finally means yes to herself."*

Because every time you drop a true No, you automatically amplify a sacred Yes—to rest, to authenticity, to joy.

Boundaries are not rejection. They're selection.

Why "Normal" Boundaries Don't Stick

Typical advice says: "Just say no and stick to it." But if your energy is still whispering *please like me,* your words are irrelevant.

A Quantum No sticks because it's not declared from fear; it's emitted from truth.

The vibe itself communicates closure—like a door that quietly locks. No slamming, no explanation, no guilt residue.

You become bored by chaos instead of enraged by it. You outgrow drama instead of fighting it.

That's maturity disguised as magic.

Witty Interlude: The Levels of No

1. **The Polite No:** "Oh gosh, thank you, but I'm swamped." (Still hoping they'll say, "You're amazing!")
2. **The Frazzled No:** "I can't keep doing everything for everyone!" (Dishwasher-slamming soundtrack optional.)
3. **The Quantum No:** Silent smile. Heart steady. Energy says it all. Others self-correct.

Upgrade accordingly.

The Body Language of Boundaries

Tension screams maybe. Relaxation whispers truth.

- Shoulders back = unavailability for chaos.
- Eye contact held = no wobble detected.
- Breath steady = "I trust myself more than your discomfort."

Your posture becomes policy.

Reflection Break:

Audit Your Boundaries in Real Time

1. Where am I saying "yes" while hoping someone cancels?
2. What situations consistently pull me into resentment loops?
3. Whose approval still makes me override my own energy?
4. What would the *Quantum No* sound—or feel— like right there?
5. Write one affirmation starting with: *"I am deliciously unavailable for..."* (fill in the blank).

Example: *I am deliciously unavailable for half-effort relationships and unpaid emotional labor.*

Stick it somewhere sacred. Bonus points for sass.

Micro-Detox Practice: Practice Tiny No's Daily

- Decline the call when you're mid-exhale.
- Let an email wait 24 hours before responding.
- Order what you actually want, not what looks "light."

- When someone demands urgency, whisper, "Not my emergency."

Micro No's build macro freedom.

Every small refusal re-tunes your frequency until your whole life feels like one enormous, easeful boundary.

The Quantum Yes Hidden Inside

Here's the paradox: the stronger your *No,* the purer your *Yes.*

Because when your energy is no longer leaking in a hundred directions, your true desires finally have room to grow.

Opportunities start matching your integrity, not your insecurity.
Relationships start mirroring your respect, not your reflex to rescue.

Your life stops feeling like constant negotiations and starts feeling like alignment.

That's the payoff of the Quantum No—it filters your reality until only truth sticks.

Final Truths

You don't owe anyone access just because they knock.
You don't have to set yourself on fire to keep anybody warm.
You don't have to narrate your worth to be believed.

Your calm is your boundary.
Your silence is your power.
Your no—clean, unapologetic, grounded—is holy.

You are the frequency.
And the frequency says: *Unavailable for bullsh*t.*

✦Chapter 13✦

Reparenting the Part of You That Had to Earn It

How to Give Yourself the Love, Permission, and Safety You've Always Been Chasing

The Child Who Learned to Hustle

Close your eyes and imagine:

A young version of you—maybe five, maybe fifteen—trying so hard to get it right.

Maybe she's cleaning her room to win approval, biting his tongue so nobody gets mad, or hiding their tears because "big kids don't cry."

Maybe they're dreaming big but learning to shrink, asking for help and hearing "do it yourself," or simply wishing, deep down, for someone to say, *You're enough, just as you are.*

This is the child who learned to hustle for love.

The one who believed, "If I'm perfect, needed, helpful, quiet, strong, or easy... maybe then I'll be safe. Maybe then I'll belong. Maybe then I'll finally be loved without conditions."

You know this part of yourself.
They still live in you.

What Is Reparenting (And Why Do We Need It)?

Reparenting is the radical act of becoming, for yourself, the loving caretaker you didn't always have.
It's not about blaming your parents or caregivers—they did what they could, with what they had.
It's about giving yourself the acceptance, protection, nurture, and permission that every human needs, but not everyone receives.

It means:

- Listening to your needs, instead of shaming them.
- Comforting your wounds, instead of denying or minimizing them.
- Encouraging your dreams, instead of clipping your wings.
- Setting boundaries, instead of exposing yourself to harm.

- Delighting in your quirks, instead of demanding you fit in.

This is not "fixing" yourself.
It's *restoring* yourself.

Why People-Pleasers Need Reparenting Most

If you learned to equate love with usefulness, performance, or invisibility, you became an expert at abandoning yourself.
You learned to:

- Ignore your intuition because someone else's mood mattered more.
- Silence your truth because peace was more valuable than honesty.
- Over-function, over-give, and over-achieve to keep the love flowing.
- Berate yourself for every "failure," real or imagined.

You became your own harshest critic—never enough, always in need of improvement.

But what if, instead, you could be your own most loyal ally?

What if you could learn to treat yourself with the kindness, patience, and compassion you once longed for?

That's what reparenting offers.

The Four Pillars of Self-Reparenting

Think of reparenting as a sturdy, loving house you build inside yourself.
Here are its four pillars:

1. Safety

You promise your inner child: "You are safe with me. I won't throw you under the bus for approval. I will protect you from situations, people, and patterns that hurt."

Practice:

- Check in with your body. Am I tense, scared, or bracing for impact?

- If yes, pause. Ask yourself, "What do I need right now to feel even 1% safer?"
- Say no to situations or people that require you to abandon yourself.

2. Nurture

You say, "Your feelings matter. I will comfort you when you're sad, scared, angry, or lost. I won't shame you for being human."

Practice:

- When you feel overwhelmed, put your hand on your heart and breathe.
- Whisper to yourself, "It's okay to feel this. I'm staying with you."
- Give yourself the rest, food, water, or soothing you'd offer a beloved child.

3. Permission

You say, "You're allowed to want, need, and dream. You don't have to earn your desires or shrink your hopes. I want more for you, not less."

Practice:

- Write down a secret wish or desire you've been hiding.
- Say aloud, "It is safe for me to want this."
- Give yourself permission to take one tiny step toward it, no matter how small.

4. Affirmation

You say, "You are enough—even when you mess up, even when you're awkward, even when you don't get it right. I delight in you. I will not abandon you."

Practice:

- List three things you love or appreciate about yourself—no qualifications or caveats.
- When you catch yourself self-criticizing, stop and say, "I'm learning. I'm growing. I'm worthy of kindness."
- Celebrate your smallest wins, no matter how trivial they seem.

Healing the Old Contracts

You may have inherited invisible "contracts" like:

- "I must keep everyone happy to stay safe."
- "My needs are a burden."
- "If I'm not exceptional, I'll be forgotten."
- "I can't trust myself to know what's best."

Reparenting means consciously breaking these contracts.
You write new ones:

- "I am allowed to disappoint others and still belong."
- "My needs are valid and manageable."
- "I am memorable for my presence, not just my performance."
- "My intuition is wise. I can trust myself."

Reflection Break:

Meeting Your Inner Child

1. What did your younger self need to hear, but rarely did?

2. When you're anxious or self-critical, what age or feeling does it remind you of?

3. How can you show up for that part of you now—with words, actions, or compassion?

4. What new promise do you want to make to your inner child, starting today?

Write it down, and let it be a living vow.

Micro-Detox Practice: The Five-Minute Reparenting Ritual

Each morning or evening, try this:

1. Find a quiet spot. Close your eyes.

2. Picture your younger self—however old feels right.

3. Imagine kneeling beside them. Place a gentle hand on their shoulder.

4. Whisper, "I see you. I love you. I will never leave you. You are enough, even when you do nothing."

5. Stay with them for five slow breaths. Notice how your body responds.

Repeat as needed.

Over time, you'll feel less alone, less frantic, less desperate for external validation.

You'll start to *belong* to yourself.

When Old Hurts Flare Up

Some days, the old wounds will ache louder. When you're tired, rejected, criticized, or stretched thin, you might slip back into old hustles—over-giving, self-blaming, shrinking.

This isn't failure.

It's a sign that your inner child needs extra care.

Pause.

Remember: You are not that powerless, lonely kid anymore.

You have you now.

Looking Forward

In the next chapter, we'll explore what it means to build relationships from this new center of self-loyalty. How to choose people who honor your fullness, how to spot the warning signs of manipulation, and how to create the kind of love and friendship that lets you grow instead of shrink.

You are the home you've always needed.
You are the parent you've been searching for.

Welcome yourself back.

Part III: The Art of Receiving & Living Unapologetically

✦Chapter 14✦

Becoming Unavailable for Performative Living

How to Drop the Masks, Stop the Auditions, and Show Up As the Real You

The Exhaustion of Pretending

There comes a moment in every healing journey when you realize:
You've spent an Olympic-level amount of energy trying to look effortless.

You weren't living — you were performing stability, performing confidence, performing empathy, performing "I'm okay."

Performative living is an adrenaline-based existence. You smile through depletion, curate your truth in bite-sized palatable captions, and collect approval like it's oxygen.

From the outside? Impressive.
On the inside? Chronic fatigue meets quiet despair.

Let's call it what it is: emotional cosplay.

The Root of the Mask

You didn't wake up one day and decide, "I'll live behind a persona."
You built your mask for protection.

As a kid, it wasn't safe to be unfiltered. Honesty cost you affection. Anger cost you belonging. So you learned the choreography of acceptability.

The problems start when the costume becomes permanent, and you forget you're wearing it.

Because masks don't just block others from seeing you—they block *you* from feeling you.

The Three Main Masks

Meet the most common disguises in the performative parade:

1. **The Competent One**
   - Emotionally bulletproof, hyper-capable, allergic to help.

- o Motto: "If I do everything right, they can't reject me."
- o Hidden wound: fear of dependence equals loss.

2. **The Chill One**
   - o Unbothered, vibey, perpetually fine.
   - o Motto: "If I don't care too much, I can't get hurt."
   - o Hidden wound: chronic self-abandonment disguised as zen.

3. **The Inspirational One**
   - o Always turning pain into content.
   - o Motto: "If I make meaning fast enough, no one will see I'm still bleeding."
   - o Hidden wound: terror of being seen mid-mess.

Notice which mask tingles when you read it. That's your healing portal.

Performance vs Presence

Performance asks, *"How do I look while doing this?"* Presence asks, *"How does this feel while I'm doing it?"*

Performance lives in mirrors.
Presence lives in the body.

When you're performing, your awareness hovers outside yourself, constantly monitoring reactions. When you're present, your energy returns home to your own skin.

Presence isn't sloppy or self-absorbed—it's sanity.

The Biology of Authenticity

Here's a fun scientific twist: your nervous system can tell when you're faking it.

Pretending safety while suppressing truth keeps the stress cycle half-activated. That's why your shoulders ache after "being nice" or your stomach knots after laughing off something that actually hurt.

Authenticity literally regulates your physiology. Honesty is parasympathetic.

Each time you drop the act, your body exhales, "Finally, reality!"

The Energetics of Non-Performance

Performative living hums at a high-frequency buzz:
restless, forward-tilted, slightly desperate.
Authenticity hums low and grounded, like a bass note.

When you stop performing:

- Your conversations slow down.
- Your laugh gets uglier (and funnier).
- Your energy returns from future tripping to present truth.

People can feel the difference. Real is magnetic—it gives permission.

You don't have to be relatable; you just have to be *real*.

The Detox: Ending Your Emotional Auditions

You've auditioned for roles like: "The Good One,"
"The Chill Friend," "The Perfect Partner."
Spoiler: None of those parts pays well.

It's time to fire your inner casting director.

Every time you catch yourself reaching for a persona, pause and ask:

"Am I performing to connect, or performing to prevent rejection?"

If it's the second, take a breath and let silence fill the gap you'd usually jam with pleasantries.

Your authenticity doesn't need rehearsals—it needs permission.

The Social Media Mirage

Let's address the glitter elephant in the room: Online life rewards performance. The algorithm loves pretend peace, curated vulnerability, "just me being raw" posts requiring 47 takes.

It's okay. We all do it. But don't confuse visibility with intimacy.

Post if you want—but make sure the version of you behind the screen still has a pulse, messy handwriting, and friendships that require no filters or ring lights.

The goal isn't to delete your platforms.
It's to stop deleting your humanity on them.

Reparenting Applied: The Internal Stage

Remember the child who had to earn love? She became the adult who performs to prove it.

Now that you're the parent, you get to rewrite the script:

"We no longer have to audition for belonging.
We already live backstage."

Reparenting here means giving yourself approval before performing for it.

The Sass & Truth Section: Spot the Performance

Let's play a game called *Who's Talking?*

When you say:

- "No worries, it's fine!" (but it's not)… that's **Mascot Energy.**

- "I'm just busy!" (but really numb)... that's **Avoidance Energy.**
- "I'm growing sooo much from this heartbreak." (an hour after it happened)... that's **Narrator Energy.**

The fix?

Pause. Feel. Don't brand it yet.

Let your life raw load before you edit the highlight reel.

Reflection Break:

Unmasking Inventory

1. Where in my life do I still feel like I'm "on"?
2. Who or what triggers my need to perform?
3. What emotion would surface if I stopped managing impressions for one day?
4. Which parts of me feel safest only when hidden?
5. Complete this line:

   "I'm becoming joyfully unavailable for performing _____."

(Examples: perfection, peacekeeping, enlightenment, coolness.)

Micro-Detox Practice: The 24-Hour Authenticity Challenge

For one full day:

- Answer honestly when someone asks, "How are you?"—without drama, just truth.
- Resist softening your tone to make others comfortable.
- Delete one "strategic" apology.
- Post nothing performative.
- Let at least one silence stretch an extra beat longer than normal.

Notice how much energy returns. Notice who leans in closer when mask-you disappears.

That's data—not everyone deserves the unscripted version, but the right ones can't love you any other way.

The Paradox of Realness

The fear says: *"If I drop the mask, they'll leave."*
Reality says: *"If I keep the mask, I'll leave myself."*

And when you truly stay with yourself—your people find you by resonance, not recruitment.

Authenticity thins the crowd but deepens the connections.

Final Truths

You are not required to be digestible to be lovable.
You are not a TED Talk, a brand, or anyone's moral mascot.
You are a living contradiction—soft and boundary-strong, silly and wise, light and shadow.

When you show up raw, you stop chasing belonging and start embodying it.

No more auditioning.
No more pretending calm while you crumble.
No more contorting into algorithms or expectations.

You're not the performance;
you're the pulse behind it.

✦Chapter 15✦

Let Love In

The Scary, Sacred Practice of

Receiving (Without Working for It)

The Awkward Art of Softening

You've done the hard stuff: detoxed the drama,
rewired your nervous system, set the boundaries,
stopped auditioning.
Now for the hardest part yet—**receiving.**

Not chasing.
Not earning.
Not scripting the thank-you in advance.
Just letting it land.

That shouldn't sound revolutionary, but for anyone
who grew up equating love with effort, *receiving* feels
like a pop quiz you never studied for.

Your body flinches.
Your brain whispers, *"I owe them something."*
Your impulse is to give it back before you get attached.

Welcome to the tender battlefield called **intimacy.**

Why Receiving Feels Dangerous

Our attachment wiring is thrifty: it recycles old data. So when comfort once came with conditions—"Good girl," "Be helpful," "Don't cry"—the nervous system learned that love has fine print.

Now, when someone offers genuine care, your alarms misfire. The body braces for the invoice.

This is why compliments make you blush-deflect ("Oh, this old thing?"), and why support feels like loss of control ("I'll just handle it myself").

Your system still believes *safety = independence.* But true connection requires interdependence—the courageous act of letting someone else's generosity touch you.

The Anatomy of Healthy Receiving

Real receiving is not passive; it's **participatory surrender.**

It looks like:

- Holding eye contact when someone praises you.
- Allowing help without repaying it instantly.
- Letting silence absorb kindness before deflecting.
- Feeling gratitude in your body instead of intellectualizing it.

It's choosing to stay open even when your reflex says, *"Duck."*

Receiving rewires survival code.
Each time you let love in, you teach your nervous system a new equation:

Love ≠ debt.
Love = exchange of energy where both expand.

The "Earned Love" Addiction

Let's talk withdrawal symptoms.

When you've built self-worth on usefulness, stillness feels like guilt. You get high on fixing, producing, gifting, rescuing—because that's when the dopamine of dignity hits.

The moment life offers you something unearned, panic barges in: *"Quick, find a chore!"*

That's the **earned-love addiction**—a chemical craving for justification.

The antidote?
Radical receptivity.
Practice letting compliments, support, abundance, and affection exist *without counter-offering performance.*

It will feel wrong at first. That's the nervous system detoxing from scarcity.

The Somatics of Receiving

Try this:
When someone offers you love—words, help, touch, opportunity—notice your first body impulse.
Do you tense, minimize, joke, change the subject?

Pause.
Inhale into the heart space.
Let the exhale say internally, *"It's safe to receive."*

Imagine love landing as warmth, not weight. Receiving is literally a parasympathetic act—it activates safety chemistry.

You can't logic your way into belonging; you have to *feel* your way there.

The Spiritual Physics of Allowing

The universe works by flow, not hoarding. What you resist receiving, you also restrict giving.

Energy can't move one-way.
By softening into acceptance, you become a conduit, not a dam.

This is why generosity sometimes dries up after burnout—you can't pour when the inlet valve is rusted shut.

Flow = give & receive.
Control = stall.

Love needs circulation. Let it move through.

The Guilt Mirage

Here's the lie: "If I receive easily, I'm selfish."

Here's the truth: refusing to receive is also imbalance. It robs the giver of fulfillment and the universe of flow.

Think of it this way—when someone compliments you, and you deflect, you return their gift unopened.

Try saying simply: "Thank you."
That's spiritual adulthood: graciousness without recoil.

Receiving in Relationships

Real intimacy isn't two people trading effort points; it's mutual allowance.

When you stop keeping emotional score, love grows oxygen.
Your partner, friend, or chosen family gets to show up fully—and you, finally, believe them when they do.

Let people love you imperfectly.

Let kindness be messy.

Let support be enough.

Perfectionism is the bouncer at the door of connection. Fire it.

Reflection Break:

The Receiving Audit

1. What emotions surface when someone gives to me with no strings?
2. Where do I downplay my needs to appear low-maintenance?
3. What compliment do I still can't accept without deflection—and why?
4. How does my body react to being cared for?
5. Finish this line:

   "I'm learning that rest, pleasure, and being loved are not rewards—they're my birthrights."

Micro-Detox Practice: The 10-Second Receive

For the next week, when something comes your way—praise, help, joy—do nothing for ten seconds.
No returning compliment. No guilt. No explanation.

Just breathe it in.
Let it land.
Feel deserving on a cellular level.

That's the muscle of allowing—it trembles only because it's new.

The Holy Permission

Authentic receiving is holy. It declares:

"I'm worthy of life showing up *without prerequisites.*"

You stop auditioning for grace and start embodying it.
You realize love was never a wage—it was always weather.

You can't force sunlight; you stand where it shines.

That's the practice.

Closing Truths

You cannot truly give from depletion or love from defense.
Receiving is not the opposite of strength—it's how strength replenishes.

Let love in.
Let compliments stay unrefunded.
Let help be holy, not humiliating.

That's not passivity—it's partnership with life.

You've earned nothing, and yet—you deserve everything aligned.

✦Chapter 16✦

Surviving the Detox Hangover

Guilt, Grief, and the Wild Relief of Choosing Yourself

The Come-Down After Boundaries

Let's be honest: healing feels amazing... *for about ten minutes.*

Then the crash lands.
After the adrenaline of breakthroughs, you wake up to an emotional hangover — less champagne sparkle, more "What have I done?"

You've said the Quantum No, stopped performing, started receiving.
Now the ghosts show up: guilt, sadness, disbelief.

This is the **Detox Hangover** — the uneasy emptiness that follows empowerment.
It's your nervous system catching up with your new choices.

Old you ran on chaos, cortisol, and compliance.
New you runs on calm and self-respect.
And calm, at first, feels like *absence*.

Guilt: The Ghost of the Old Contract

Every time you choose yourself, guilt will knock and say, "Um, hi, we've never done it this way."

That's not morality — that's muscle memory.
Guilt isn't proof you're wrong; it's proof you're rewiring.

You spent years worshipping other people's comfort.
Of course, it feels criminal now to prioritize yours.

When guilt hits, breathe and narrate what's happening:

"This is discomfort, not danger.
My body is adjusting to freedom."

Eventually, guilt stops sounding like conscience and more like what it truly is: withdrawal from self-betrayal.

Grief: The Price of Peace

The unsung stage of healing is grief — not only for people lost, but for *versions* of you lost.

You grieve the performer, the pleaser, the rescuer.
You grieve the friendships that only survived under over-giving.
You even grieve the chaos — because it felt familiar.

Let the mourning happen.
You're not being dramatic; you're metabolizing memory.

Saying goodbye to an identity is still a breakup.

Tears are just your nervous system's water ceremony.

The Paradox of Relief

Alongside guilt and grief hides something shocking: *relief.*

A quiet, delicious ease that whispers, "I can breathe again."

It feels suspicious at first — you'll try to ruin it just to restore the familiar struggle.
Don't. Stay bored.

Relief is not laziness; it's life coming back online.

You're not unmotivated — you're de-traumatized.

Why Healing Feels Lonely

When your vibration changes, your audience thins.
People used to your compliance may interpret your calm as cold.

They're reading a new frequency without subtitles.

It's okay. You're not being abandoned; you're being refined.
There will be a gap between the old you and the future you, and that gap is where loneliness lives.

Fill it with presence, not panic.
This is where self-trust grows roots.

Nervous System Detox 101

The hangover stage has three main sensations:

1. **Flatness** – You're not depressed; you're under-stimulated. Adrenaline withdrawal creates emotional quiet.
   Prescription: simplicity, sunlight, hydration, small joys.
2. **Doubt** – "Maybe I overreacted." No, you just aren't used to peace yet.
   Prescription: remember how predictable chaos felt and honor your choice to exit it.
3. **Craving** – You miss intensity. That's biochemical, not destiny.
   Prescription: replace drama dopamine with movement, art, laughter.

Repatterning is rehab for the nervous system—it shakes, sweats, then stabilizes.

When Healing Feels Like Regression

You'll have days where you relapse into old coping. Cool. That's integration, not failure.

Imagine your growth like spiral stairs—you revisit old floors, but from higher levels.

Every time you catch yourself mid-pattern and self-correct faster, that's mastery.

You're not backsliding; you're re-learning with witness consciousness.

Reflection Break:

The Emotional Debrief

1. What emotions keep surfacing since I began setting real boundaries?
2. Where do I still equate comfort with danger?
3. Which relationships feel different now, and how might I release without resentment?
4. What part of me misses chaos, and what need was chaos meeting?
5. Complete this truth:

   "I am allowed to feel horrible on the way to feeling free."

Micro-Detox Practice: The Guilt Flip

Every time guilt shows up this week, pause and rephrase:

- Old script: *"I'm selfish."*
- New script: *"I'm self-honoring."*
- Old script: *"I'm closing doors."*
- New script: *"I'm clearing hallways."*

Keep a running list called **Evidence of Peace** —
moments when life feels easier, simpler, lighter.
That's your rehab diary.

The Wild Relief of Choosing Yourself

Here's the plot twist no one tells you: self-loyalty feels
euphoric once the dust settles.
The world doesn't collapse when you stop managing
everyone else's comfort.
You get time, energy, dignity back.

Freedom tastes electric, like biting into weather.

Yes, guilt lingers. Yes, grief visits.
But underneath them hums the sound of alignment.

That hum? That's peace warming up.

Closing Truths

Healing is not linear—it's detox.
First the purge, then the craving, then the calm.

You will survive the emotional hangover.
You will stop missing what drained you.
You will stop apologizing for not drowning politely.

Guilt fades. Grief softens.
Relief remains.

And on the other side of all three?
Clarity.

✦Chapter 17✦

Cord-Cutting, Field-Holding, and the Energetic Upgrade

Recovering Your Power and Reclaiming Your Field

The Invisible Hangover

You've cleaned out the people-pleasing, survived the guilt detox, maybe even matched your breath to your boundaries—and yet, you still feel *tethered*.

You wake up thinking about people you don't even talk to anymore.
Their tone still plays in your head.
You feel their weight in your energy even when your phone is blessedly silent.

That's not obsession. That's **energetic residue.**

Healing the body and mind is step one; healing the *field* is how you graduate.

What Cords Actually Are

Forget the spooky imagery—energetic cords are simply channels of emotional data exchange. They form whenever sustained attention or attachment links you to another's field.

They aren't "evil"; they're informational. But when the relationship ends or stagnates, those cords can drain bandwidth like unseen open browser tabs.

Cord-cutting isn't a punishment; it's **closing outdated energetic contracts.**

Emotional Wi-Fi and Boundaries

Think of your energy field like Wi-Fi. Whoever has the password can ping your system. Old lovers, family trauma, work politics—each unfinished loop keeps pulling notifications.

Field-holding means changing the password and finally owning your router.

You can still have empathy; you just don't have open access ports.

The goal isn't isolation; it's intentional signal.

The Somatics of Energy Leaks

You'll know you're leaking energy when:

- You run imaginary arguments in your head.
- You feel inexplicably tired after thinking of someone.
- Your emotions swing based on others' moods.
- You can't stop checking a phone that never rings.

Those aren't moral flaws—they're resonance echoes. Energy is sticky; thoughts are cords.

The antidote? Awareness, breath, and sovereignty.

Cord-Cutting Ritual (Modern Version)

Skip the drama candles if they're not your thing; this is nervous-system physics.

1. **Ground.**
   Sit, breathe, anchor in your body. Imagine roots in earth or weight in chair.
2. **Identify the Connection.**
   Bring to mind the person/situation that still

feels latched. Name the feeling it carries—grief, guilt, addiction to closure.

3. **Visualize the Channel.**
Picture a light cord between you. No right or wrong look—just see the link.

4. **Return Energy Home.**
With compassion, say:

"I release you to your path and call my energy back cleansed and whole."

5. **Seal the Field.**
Imagine a luminous layer around your body: permeable to truth, impermeable to chaos.

6. **Breathe Until Neutral.**
You'll know it's done when your body feels *quiet*.

Cord-cutting is frequency hygiene; it's deleting old data caches.

Field-Holding 101

After cutting cords, you build containment.
This is the art of keeping your energy steady, *no matter who walks in the room.*

Practically, it looks like:

- Centering before social events.
- Grounding after intense conversations.
- Choosing response over reaction.
- Becoming the calm one without rescuing.

You stop mirroring everyone—you start anchoring everyone, by example.

That's **field leadership,** not control.

The Energetic Upgrade

Once you stop siphoning energy into outdated cords, your frequency recalibrates.

Symptoms of upgrade:

- Spontaneous joy without reason.
- Faster manifestation (because less interference).
- Irritation toward superficial interactions (normal).
- Random impulse to declutter everything (listen to it).

You're not "above" others; you're simply resonating cleaner.

Space once filled by obsession becomes creative potential.

Don't Mistake Detachment for Disconnection

Cutting cords doesn't mean cutting compassion.
You can bless someone and still block their number.
You can love from afar and still guard your bandwidth.

True detachment is intimacy without enmeshment— loving without leaking.

Reflection Break:

Field Inventory

1. Who or what still feels plugged into my energy?
2. Which thoughts loop daily, and what emotion powers them?
3. When do I feel drained that doesn't match physical effort?

4. What new boundaries would protect my frequency?

5. Write this declaration:

"I reclaim my energy from every space I no longer belong in.
My field is sovereign, my love still intact."

Micro-Detox Practice: Daily Reclaim

Before bed, whisper:

"Anything that's mine, return to me clean.
Anything that's not, return to Source with peace."

Then imagine a light sweep through your auric Wi-Fi.

It takes less than a minute, but the sleep difference is wild.

The Physics of Power Return

When energy is fragmented among old attachments, manifestation gets garbled—like multiple radio stations at once.

As you reclaim fragments, your signal sharpens. Intentions manifest faster not because you're magic, but because you're finally **undiluted.**

Power is just coherent attention.

Closing Truths

Cord-cutting isn't about vengeance; it's about voltage. You are not cold for conserving energy— you are wise for maintaining current.

Your job is not to heal everyone you've ever touched; it's to steward the frequency that heals by example.

Now your energy isn't borrowed—it's embodied.

You own your field.
And once your field is reclaimed, the next question becomes: how do you stay open within it?

✦Chapter 18✦

Choosing Relationships That Honor Your Fullness

How to Build Connections Where You Can Be Fully, Fiercely Yourself

From Self-Healing to Relational Truth

You've done the inner work: reparenting, regulating, cutting outdated cords.
You're no longer performing for belonging.

Now comes the next sacred challenge — being *seen* in your wholeness and letting that wholeness shape your relationships.

Because healing in isolation can only take you so far. Freedom wants witness. And the nervous system learns safety most powerfully through *healthy connection.*

Safe vs Familiar

Your body knows the difference — even before your mind does.

- **Familiar** is what your system recognizes, even if it's painful: caretaking, fixing, staying small to keep the peace.
- **Safe** is what allows your system to expand, speak truth, and breathe fully.

For the recovering peacekeeper, *safe* can initially feel boring or scary.
That's just recalibration. You're not losing spark; you're learning stability.

When you feel uneasy in goodness, that's the sound of old patterns unplugging.

The Shrink Test

Notice where your energy contracts:

- You self-edit mid-sentence.
- Your "no" is punished or ignored.
- You're praised for productivity, not presence. Wherever you must shrink to belong, you're not in love — you're in survival.

The Expansion Signals

Now contrast that with relationships that let you breathe:

- You leave lighter, not leakier.
- Boundaries land without backlash.
- Curiosity replaces competition.
- Conflict repairs deeper trust.
- Your weirdness, brilliance, and sensitivity are met with **"More of that, please."**

That's what real belonging feels like: *roominess inside your own skin.*

Building the Courage to Choose Differently

Choosing aligned connections requires a new form of bravery:

1. **Tolerate the gap.** Some people will fade when you stop auditioning. Let them.
2. **Stay visible anyway.** Don't dim just because your glow isn't everyone's taste.

3. **Risk honest intimacy.** You don't attract truth by performing it.
4. **Let loneliness mean spaciousness — not failure.**

Your people will recognize you by resonance, not résumé.

When Family or Old Friends Don't Get It

You can love them from a safer distance.
Lower access doesn't equal less love; it equals less leakage.
Radical acceptance sounds like:

"They may never get it, and that's okay.
I can still keep my wholeness intact."

You don't owe everyone equal access, especially to the tender parts you fought to reclaim.

Reflection Break: Inventory of Belonging

1. Who in my life feels like exhale, not performance?

2. Where do I still shrink to stay chosen?

3. Which relationships are ready for honest conversation, and which are ready for gentle closure?

4. What kind of connection makes my nervous system hum, not buzz?

Write your vision of *expansive belonging* — how it looks, sounds, and feels.

Micro-Practice: The Fullness Check-In

After each interaction, ask:

"Did I feel free or filtered?"
"Did I leave more alive or more depleted?"

No judgment — just data. Awareness changes momentum.

✦Chapter 19✦

Radical Boundaries: What Actually Happens When You Set Them

The Fallout, the Freedom, and the New Circle of Belonging

The Myth of Clean Endings

Everyone loves the aesthetic of boundaries until they start working.
Then things get noisy.

When you finally say *no*, people hear *never*.
When you choose rest, they see rebellion.
When you stop rescuing, they accuse you of coldness.

Congratulations — your healing just went public.

Boundaries are not rejection; they're **clarity with consequences.**
And clarity shakes loose every interaction that relied on confusion.

The Initial Fallout

Here's the honest roll-out:

- Some people will get defensive because your compliance secretly benefited them.
- Others will disappear quietly — not villains, just complete.
- A few will adjust, respect you more, and stay.

Don't personalize the purge; it's energetic housekeeping.

Every system resists change before it reorganizes.

Why Boundaries Trigger Fear

Your nervous system equates boundaries with danger because, once, speaking the truth *was* punished.
But this time, the threat is remembered, not real.

When you set a limit and feel shaky after, that's your inner child scanning for fallout.
Let the adult-you reassure:

"This is allowed. No one gets hurt when I tell the truth."

The adrenaline will fade. The self-trust will stay.

The Lonely Middle

Between losing old roles and meeting new resonance, there's emptiness — the *Boundary Void.*
It feels like exile, but it's actually incubation.

Think of it as moving apartments before your new address gets furniture.

In the void:

- You doubt yourself.
- You romanticize the chaos you left.
- You almost text The Unavailable One™.

Don't. Sit still. Let the void do its work.

You're not being punished — you're being purified for right-fit belonging.

Boundary Fatigue

At some point, you'll whine, "I'm tired of holding lines."
Totally fair. In early stages, boundaries are cognitive — you have to *remember* them.

Eventually, they become **energetic posture** — lived, not memorized.

Healthy boundaries don't require guarding 24/7; they emit a quiet signal.
People feel what's permissible before you announce it.

That's when boundaries become natural law.

The Social Physics of Boundaries

Every boundary rearranges your orbit.
When you stop over-functioning, the over-dependent must evolve or fall away.
When you stop absorbing projection, gossip loses gravity.
When you stop apologizing for space, respect fills the vacuum.

At first, you'll mourn the collapse. Then you'll realize:
Nothing real ever leaves.
Only contracts expired by growth.

The New Circle of Belonging

What emerges after the void is extraordinary: Relationships based on mutual regulation, not manipulation.

You'll notice conversations that feel like breathing instead of bracing.
You'll experience love that asks questions instead of compliance.
You'll meet people who don't need access to prove closeness.

This is your **aligned tribe** — peace-literate, truth-friendly, respect-fluent.

To recognize them, you must be one of them. And you are now.

Reflection Break:

Boundary Inventory

1. Where do I still bargain for peace by shrinking?
2. Which relationship actually improved once limits were honest?

3. What "no" still needs saying — to others or to myself?

4. What scares me more: rejection or self-betrayal?

5. Finish this truth:

   "My boundaries aren't walls; they're doors with selective entry."

The Freedom Phase

Once guilt subsides, boundaries feel less like defense and more like design.
You suddenly have time, space, and inner silence.

That isn't loneliness. That's **available bandwidth.**

Use it to create, rest, love well, and listen inward.
That's why you cleared the noise—to finally hear yourself.

Closing Truths

Boundaries aren't endings; they're architecture for honest relating.

They reveal who's capable of real intimacy—and who only wanted access, not connection.

You will survive the fallout.
You will outgrow the guilt.
You will magnetize the aligned.

That's the circle that forms around your truth.

✦Chapter 20✦

The Afterglow

Living Unapologetically, Loving Authentically, and Shaping a New Legacy

Arrival Isn't a Moment — It's a Tone

The afterglow isn't fireworks; it's steadiness.

It's waking up unarmored.
It's laughter that doesn't perform.
It's silence that feels safe, not empty.

After years of fixing, performing, detoxing, and pruning, you start existing in your own frequency. That frequency is peace with texture — joy that doesn't demand an audience.

Congratulations. You're home.

The Texture of Authentic Peace

Real peace isn't sparkly or mood-board tidy.
It's the slow burn of congruence — being the same on the inside as you appear outside.

Peace sounds like:

- Saying "No, thank you" without a heart race.
- Letting love land without guilt.
- Trusting silence.
- Belly laughter that comes from safety, not sarcasm.

This is the nervous system's version of sunrise.

The Unlearning of Apology

You spent a lifetime apologizing for being too much, then another spent apologizing for needing less. The afterglow is neutrality: you stop apologizing altogether.

You realize that existing with integrity is not arrogance — it's alignment.

Apology becomes sacred again, reserved for repair, not self-erasure.

That's emotional adulthood.

The New Definition of Legacy

Legacy used to mean what you build for others to remember you by.
Now it means **how cleanly your energy ripples through the people you love.**

Your healed nervous system becomes generational wealth.
Your calm becomes pattern-breaking medicine.
Your authenticity teaches by resonance more than by lesson.

That's the quiet revolution—micro, yet massive.

Loving from Wholeness

When you stop chasing validation, love becomes choice, not evidence.
You no longer perform affection to buy security; you share it because security's internal.

Loving authentically means:

- Listening without rescuing.
- Holding space while honoring self.

- Letting people have their path without folding into theirs.

You no longer fear loss because you no longer equate it with abandonment.

The Subtle Glow

The afterglow doesn't announce itself; others notice it first.
They ask, *"What changed?"*
You smile, shrug, and say, *"I got quiet."*

Light no longer requires a spotlight; it radiates inward-out — stable, not showy.

You've become the calm you used to seek.

Reflection Break:

Legacy Questions

1. What behaviors now feel too expensive for my peace?
2. Where do I still unconsciously shrink for comfort's sake?
3. Who flourishes in my presence now—and do I?

4. What ripple am I choosing to send forward each day?

5. Complete this line:

   "My legacy is nervous-system safety disguised as love."

Micro-Practice: The Daily Return

Each night, whisper:

"Today, I lived aligned enough."

No score-keeping, no spiritual grading.
Just a reminder that growth is now default, not project.

The Final Integration

Healing was never about becoming invincible.
It was about remembering you're inherently intact.

You'll still have moods, heartbreaks, and moments of regression.
But the difference now?
You return to self-faster.

That's mastery.

Conclusion
The New Map: Walking Forward as Your Own North Star

Here we are—the other side of the detox. The applause has faded, the people-pleasing has cracked open, the masks have slipped off one by one, and what's left is *you*. No performance. No audition. No gold stars to collect. Just the raw, luminous truth of someone learning—maybe for the first time—to navigate life by their own inner compass.

Let's take a breath here. Feel that? That steadiness is yours. You built it.

This journey wasn't about becoming invincible or "fixed." It was about remembering the wholeness that's been humming underneath all along. The part of you that existed before the praise, before the perfectionism, before you learned to measure your worth in reactions. That essence never left—it just got buried under all the "shoulds," the survival strategies, the stories other people wrote on your skin.

You've sifted through them now. And piece by piece, you've reclaimed yourself.

The Old Map: External GPS

For so long, you were guided by everyone else's coordinates.
Their comfort. Their opinions. Their applause.
You built your sense of direction off external feedback—constantly correcting course to avoid rejection, scanning the horizon for permission to breathe or bloom.

But that map—while familiar—was never drawn for *you*. It kept you looping through the same emotional country: guilt, exhaustion, invisibility, repeat. You mistook survival routes for belonging trails.

And still, you made it here.
That means you already know how to navigate chaos.
What you're learning now is how to navigate *peace*.

The New Map: Internal Compass

On the new map, there are fewer landmarks and fewer guarantees—but infinitely more freedom.
Here, the directions sound like:

- "Pause before you people-please."

- "If it drains your joy, it costs too much."
- "When in doubt, return to your body—it tells the truth faster than your brain ever will."
- "Rest is not withdrawal; it's recalibration."
- "You don't need to prove your wholeness. Just live it."

Out there, love and approval were conditional, rationed out based on performance.
In here, love becomes gravity—quiet, constant, and unearned.

You'll still have moments when the old GPS starts yelling: "Rerouting! Apologize! Over-explain! Make them comfortable!"
Let it glitch.
Smile.
You're driving now.

Walking Forward as Your Own North Star

Being your own North Star isn't about knowing every answer. It's about trusting that you can adjust, that you can meet yourself honestly, that you can self-correct without self-abandonment. You'll keep evolving the map as you go, drawing new borders around your peace, redesigning your relationships from truth instead of tension.

The more you listen inward, the quieter the outer noise becomes. The more you follow what feels coherent instead of what looks impressive, the more magnetic your life gets—not in a showy way, but in a steady, heart-level way.

Your North Star lives in your nervous system now—in every deep breath after a clean "no," in every slow exhale after allowing yourself to receive, in every moment you stay present when the urge to perform hums loud and familiar.

It's in the silence you no longer fear.
It's in the boundaries that no longer need defending.
It's in the joy that doesn't have to be justified.

What Freedom Actually Feels Like

Freedom isn't fireworks—it's the absence of panic. It's drinking your morning coffee without mentally rehearsing apologies.

It's laughter that doesn't come from relief but from resonance.

It's intimacy that doesn't need explanation or proof.

It's choosing rest without guilt, boundaries without blame, and love without performance.

You will backslide sometimes. Everyone does. You'll find yourself over-explaining, smoothing, replaying old roles. But the difference now is, you'll notice.

You'll pause. You'll choose again.

That's mastery—not perfection, but presence.

The Legacy of Self-Trust

By walking this path, you've done something radical—you've created a new emotional lineage. Generations behind you were taught to survive by pleasing; generations ahead will learn to thrive by trusting.

You've ended something ancient. You've begun something luminous.

Every time you honor your truth, you leave a breadcrumb trail for someone else who's still lost in the maze of earning love.

Every time you choose rest over rushing, boundaries

over burnout, honesty over safety, you extend a quiet invitation: *Come home. It's safe here now.*

Your Only Assignment from Here

Don't make this your next project.
Let it be your practice.

Keep listening. Keep choosing. Keep softening.
Let love land, again and again, in all the awkward,
holy places it once couldn't reach.

When you forget, come back to one simple question:

"What would I do if I already believed I was enough?"

Then do that.

Over and over, until it feels like the truth.

Because it is.

You are your own North Star now—steady, embodied,
and brilliantly uncensored.
Navigate from there, and every path becomes home.

Bonus Section

Journal Prompts for Recovering People-Pleasers

Because clarity is healing, and truth is the doorway to self-return.

Use these prompts when you feel yourself slipping into old patterns—or anytime you want to check in with the version of you that no longer needs to prove anything.

1. What am I afraid will happen if I say no? And what part of me learned that?
2. When was the last time I said yes, but really meant no? What would I do differently now?
3. Whose approval do I still find myself craving, even subtly? Why?
4. What do I believe I have to *do* in order to be loved? Where did that belief come from?
5. What do I need to tell the child inside me who thought love had to be earned?
6. How does it feel in my body when I'm abandoning myself?

7. What would it look like to trust that I am enough—even if no one else claps?

8. What version of me do I want to protect? And what version am I ready to release?

Write like nobody's watching. Then read it back like you're holding the hand of someone you're learning to love again—*you*.

Reclaiming Ritual: Burn the Old Scripts

A symbolic practice to release the roles, rules, and responsibilities that were never yours to carry.

You'll need:

- A quiet space
- Paper and pen
- A safe fireproof bowl, fireplace, or outdoor setting
- A lighter or match
- Optional: calming music, a blanket, or a supportive friend

Instructions:

1. Write down every identity, role, or rule you've been performing for approval.
   - "I must always be nice."
   - "I can't disappoint people."
   - "I have to earn love."
   - "If I speak up, I'll lose connection."
   - "My worth comes from being needed."
2. Read them aloud—softly, clearly, one at a time.
3. Then, one by one, *burn them*. Watch the flame do what your body has been aching to do— **release**.
4. As each script turns to ash, say:

   "I release the need to perform for love.
   I return to the truth of who I am."

5. When finished, take a deep breath. Place your hand on your chest and say:

   "I belong. I am whole. I am home."

Optional: Scatter the ashes outdoors or bury them as a symbolic burial of the roles that once kept you small.

Mantras for Belonging Without Performance

Affirmations to anchor your nervous system in truth—especially when the urge to please, prove, or perform returns.

Repeat these aloud, whisper them, write them in your journal, or place them where you'll see them often.

I don't need to earn rest.
I don't need to perform for love.
I belong, even when I disappoint people.
My boundaries are acts of self-trust, not rejection.
I can be messy and still be worthy.
I release the need to be palatable.
I choose truth over likeability.
I trust that the real me is enough.
I do not owe anyone an edited version of myself.
I am loved—not for being easy, but for being *me*.

Say them slowly. Let them echo. These aren't just words. They're recalibrations. They're *reminders of what's always been true.*

References

Beattie, M. (1986). *Codependent no more: How to stop controlling others and start caring for yourself.* Hazelden Publishing.

Braiker, H. B. (2001). *The disease to please: Curing the people-pleasing syndrome.* McGraw-Hill.

Brown, B. (2010). *The gifts of imperfection: Let go of who you think you're supposed to be and embrace who you are.* Hazelden Publishing.

Brown, B. (2012). *Daring greatly: How the courage to be vulnerable transforms the way we live, love, parent, and lead.* Gotham Books.

Brown, B. (2021). *Atlas of the heart: Mapping meaningful connection and the language of human experience.* Random House.

Dispenza, J. (2014). *You are the placebo: Making your mind matter.* Hay House.

Haemmerle, J., & Lindsley, J. (2023). *Energetic boundaries: Practical tools for sensitivity and self-leadership.* Sounds True.

Hooks, b. (2000). *All about love: New visions.* William Morrow Paperbacks.

LePera, N. (2021). *How to do the work: Recognize your patterns, heal from your past, and create yourself.* Harper Wave.

Maté, G. (2003). *When the body says no: Exploring the stress-disease connection.* Vintage Canada.

Mohr, T. (2014). *Playing big: Practical wisdom for women who want to speak up, create, and lead.* Portfolio.

Neff, K. (2011). *Self-compassion: The proven power of being kind to yourself.* William Morrow.

Porges, S. W. (2017). *The pocket guide to the polyvagal theory: The transformative power of feeling safe.* W. W. Norton & Company.

Tawwab, N. G. (2021). *Set boundaries, find peace: A guide to reclaiming yourself.* Tarcher Perigee.

Tolle, E. (2005). *A new earth: Awakening to your life's purpose.* Penguin Group.

van der Kolk, B. A. (2014). *The body keeps the score: Brain, mind, and body in the healing of trauma.* Viking.

Watts, A. (1951). *The wisdom of insecurity: A message for an age of anxiety.* Vintage Books.

Weiss, H., & De Young, B. (2020). *The self-healer's journal: Guided prompts to help you move beyond trauma and become your own badass self.* Rockridge Press.

Additional foundational works in social and relational psychology:

Bowlby, J. (1969). *Attachment and loss: Vol. 1. Attach ment.* Basic Books.

Festinger, L. (1954). A theory of social comparison pro cesses. *Human Relations, 7*(2), 117–140. https://doi.org/10.1177/001872675400700202

www.ingramcontent.com/pod-product-compliance
Lightning Source LLC
Chambersburg PA
CBHW051305120626
46547CB00015B/2104